Simple Patchwork

Stunning Quilts
That Are a Snap to Stitch

Kim Diehl

C&T PUBLISHING
Another Maker Inspired!

Copyright © 2020 by Kim Diehl

Publisher: Amy Barrett-Daffin

Creative Director: Gailen Runge

Senior Editor: Roxane Cerda

Cover And Book Designer: Kathy Kotomaimoce

Copy Editor: Melissa Bryan

Illustrators: Missy Shepler, Christine Erikson

Photographer: Brent Kane

Production Coordinator: Zinnia Heinzmann

Published by C&T Publishing, Inc., P.O. Box 1456, Lafayette, CA 94549

Library of Congress Control Number: 2023935790

Printed in China

10 9 8 7 6 5 4 3 2

SPECIAL THANKS

Photography for this book was taken at the home of Kirsten Yanasek (Instagram: @brightyellowdoor) of Everett, Washington, and at Minglewood Lodge in Gretna, Nebraska.

Contents

To download a free patchwork pillowcase pattern, visit
tinyurl.com/11588-patterns-download

Introduction

If you're anything like me, there are times when you enjoy a challenge and want to test your quiltmaking skills, but there are also times when it's nice to stitch something uncomplicated just for the fun of it. In that spirit, I decided to treat myself to a year of embracing simplicity and challenged myself to design a collection of patchwork projects that would be a snap to stitch without sacrificing style. Since variety is the spice of life, I made sure to include tons of projects that range from bed quilts with supersized patchwork to the occasional mini for a nice little change of pace. Best of all, this versatile mix of quilts can be used all through your home.

For experienced quiltmakers, the designs in this book present a great opportunity to sail through the patchwork steps, easily starting *and* finishing your chosen project. If you're new to quiltmaking, you'll find the projects to be super approachable and fun to stitch, while they simultaneously help build your patchwork skills.

The methods I use are simple but effective and come from being a self-taught quiltmaker. What I mean by this is that I had no one to show me the ropes and teach me the basics when I tackled my first quilt, so I figured out each new step on my own as I came to it. When I goofed something up (which happened regularly as I was learning), I would just tell myself that was one way not to do it, dust myself off, and try again until I nailed it. In hindsight, I believe this was a blessing because it enabled me to explore quiltmaking without any preconceived ideas about how things should or shouldn't be done.

Through much trial and error, I've developed a sound set of guidelines and methods that help me achieve beautiful results in my quiltmaking. Many of these practices include small details and little things that you wouldn't typically find in a "how-to-quilt" tutorial, but when you add them all together, they make a huge impact! It's my hope that they'll make a huge impact on *your* quiltmaking as well, so I've gathered together tons of these little nuggets of information and shared them with you in "Kim's Favorite Tips, Tricks, Hints, and Helps" on page 100.

I wish you many happy hours of stitching as you explore the simply pieced projects in this book. Ready ... set ... stitch!

~ Kim

Geese in the Henhouse

Supersize your patchwork and prepare for lightning-quick progress as you sew this quilt featuring a fusion of modern and classic styles. Medium and dark prints in shades of red, blue, orange, and green give the illusion of layers of color in the quilt center, and the open cream squares provide an ideal canvas to showcase beautifully stitched quilting designs.

- - - - - - - -

FINISHED QUILT SIZE
60½" × 60½"

Materials

Yardage is based on 42" of usable fabric width after prewashing and removing selvages.

- ✦ ⅞ yard of cream print for quilt-center patchwork
- ✦ 1 chubby sixteenth (9" × 10½") *each* of medium red, blue, green, and orange prints for quilt-center patchwork
- ✦ 1 chubby sixteenth *each* of dark red, blue, green, and orange prints for quilt-center patchwork
- ✦ 1 yard of black print #1 for quilt-center patchwork and binding
- ✦ 2⅜ yards of black print #2 for border patchwork
- ✦ 14 fat quarters (18" × 21") of assorted prints for border patchwork
- ✦ 3¾ yards of fabric for backing
- ✦ 67" × 67" square of batting

pin point

Fat Quarters: The 14 assorted prints called for will yield a nice blend of fabrics for the flying-geese border units, but this is merely a jumping-off point. If you'd rather have fewer leftovers, use just nine fat quarters and cut nine squares from each print. For a scrappier look, use 18 fat quarters as I did, cut 4 or 5 squares per print, and add the leftover scraps to your stash for future projects.

Cutting

Cut all pieces across the width of the fabric in the order given unless otherwise noted.

From the cream print, cut:

1 strip, 8⅞" × 42"; crosscut into 4 squares, 8⅞" × 8⅞".
   Cut each square in half diagonally *once* to yield
   2 triangles (total of 8).

2 strips, 8½" × 42"; crosscut into 8 squares,
   8½" × 8½"

From *each* of the medium chubby sixteenths, cut:

1 square, 8⅞" × 8⅞" (combined total of 4); cut each
   square in half diagonally *once* to yield 2 triangles
   (combined total of 8)

From *each* of the dark chubby sixteenths, cut:

1 square, 8½" × 8½" (combined total of 4)

From black print #1, cut:

2 strips, 8½" × 42"; crosscut into 5 squares,
   8½" × 8½". From the remainder of the second
   strip, cut 3 binding strips, 2½" × 31".*

4 additional binding strips, 2½" × 42"*

**For my chubby-binding method on page 111, reduce
the strip width to 2".*

From black print #2, cut:

14 strips, 5½" × 42"; crosscut into 40 rectangles,
   5½" × 10½". (If your fabrics haven't been
   prewashed, you may be able to cut 4 rectangles
   from each strip and reduce the number of strips
   to 10.)

From *each* of the 14 print fat quarters, cut:

6 squares, 5½" × 5½" (combined total of 84; you'll
   have 4 left over). If you've opted to use fewer or
   more fat quarters, adjust the number of squares
   cut from each print accordingly to yield the total
   number needed.

Piecing the Quilt Center

*Sew all pieces with right sides together using a ¼" seam
allowance unless otherwise noted. Press the seam
allowances as indicated by the arrows or otherwise
instructed.*

1 Layer and stitch a cream and a medium print
   8⅞" triangle along the long diagonal edges.
Press. Trim away the dog-ear points. Repeat to piece
a total of eight half-square-triangle units measuring
8½" square, including the seam allowances.

Make 8 units,
8½" × 8½".

2 Lay out two medium red half-square-triangle
   units, one dark red 8½" square, and one cream
8½" square in two horizontal rows. Join the pieces in
each row. Press. Join the rows. Press. Repeat with the
blue, green, and orange prints to piece a total of four
corner units measuring 16½" square, including the
seam allowances.

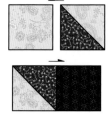

Make 4 corner units,
16½" × 16½".

3 Join a black #1 and a cream 8½" square.
   Press. Repeat to piece a total of four
black-and-cream units measuring 8½" × 16½",
including the seam allowances.

Make 4 units, 8½" × 16½".

Finished quilt size: 60½" × 60½"

DESIGNED BY *Kim Diehl*

PIECED BY *Doris Coffey*

MACHINE QUILTED BY *Connie Tabor*

4 Lay out the four corner units from step 2, the four black-and-cream units, and one 8½" black #1 square in three horizontal rows. Join the pieces in each row. Press. Join the rows. Press. The quilt center should measure 40½" square, including the seam allowances.

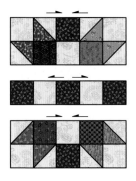
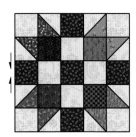

Quilt center, 40½" × 40½"

Piecing the Flying-Geese Units

1 Use a pencil and an acrylic ruler to draw a diagonal sewing line from corner to corner on the wrong side of each assorted print 5½" square.

2 Layer a prepared assorted print 5½" square onto one end of a 5½" × 10½" black #2 rectangle as shown. Stitch the pieces along the drawn line. Fold the resulting inner triangle open, aligning the corner with the corner of the black rectangle. Press. Trim away the layers beneath the top triangle, leaving a ¼" seam allowance. In the same manner, add a mirror-image triangle to the remaining end of the black rectangle, using a 5½" square of a different print. Repeat to piece a total of 40 flying-geese units measuring 5½" × 10½", including the seam allowances. You'll have four leftover assorted print squares.

Make 40 units, 5½" × 10½".

Piecing and Adding the Border

1 Lay out eight flying-geese units in one horizontal row as shown. Join the units. Press. Repeat to piece a total of four flying-geese border units measuring 10½" × 40½", including the seam allowances. Reserve the remaining flying-geese units for later use.

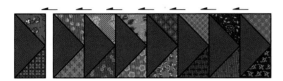

Make 4 border units, 10½" × 40½".

2 Refer to the quilt assembly diagram at right to join a flying-geese border unit to the right and left sides of the quilt center, turning the rows as needed to achieve the design. Press. Reserve the two remaining flying-geese border units for later use.

3 Join two reserved flying-geese units from step 1 as shown. Press. Repeat to piece a total of four flying-geese corner units measuring 10½" square, including the seam allowances.

Make 4 corner units, 10½" × 10½".

4 Join a flying-geese corner unit to each end of the reserved flying-geese border units from step 2. Press.

Make 2 borders, 10½" × 60½".

5 Sew the pieced borders to the remaining sides of the quilt top, turning the direction of the rows as needed to achieve the design. Press.

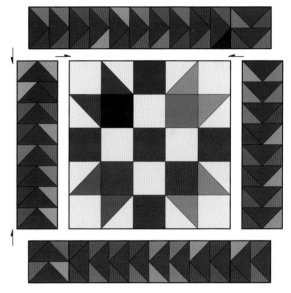

Quilt assembly

Completing the Quilt

Layer and baste the quilt top, batting, and backing. Quilt the layers. The featured quilt was machine quilted with an edge-to-edge design of curved feathers in randomly placed clusters. Referring to "Chubby Binding" on page 111, or substituting your own favorite method, use the black print #1 binding strips to bind the quilt.

Half-and-Half

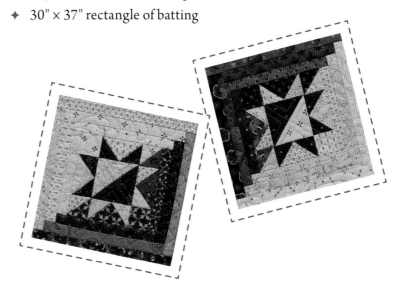

G enerations of quiltmakers have loved and stitched quilts with the classic star and courthouse step designs, so what could be better than merging these two elements into one fantastic patchwork block? Half star and half strips, these split-personality blocks bring endless setting and design opportunities to the table.

- - - - - - - -

FINISHED QUILT SIZE:
23½" × 30½"

FINISHED BLOCK SIZE:
7" × 7"

Materials

Yardage is based on 42" of usable fabric width after prewashing and removing selvages.

- ✦ 6 charm squares (5" × 5") of assorted red prints for blocks
- ✦ ½ yard *total* of assorted medium and dark print scraps for blocks
- ✦ 6 fat eighths (9" × 21") of assorted cream prints for blocks
- ✦ ⅛ yard of gold print for border #1
- ✦ ½ yard of black print for border #2 and binding
- ✦ 1½" × 19½" strip *each* of 2 different teal prints for border #2
- ✦ ¼ yard of plum print for border #3
- ✦ 1½" × 23½" strip *each* of 2 different burnt-orange prints for border #3
- ✦ ¼ yard of brown print for border #4
- ✦ ⅞ yard of fabric for backing
- ✦ 30" × 37" rectangle of batting

Cutting

Cut all pieces across the width of the fabric in the order given unless otherwise noted. As I worked on my quilt, I found it easiest to choose and cut one set of A and B pieces from the assorted prints for the background areas behind the cream star points for each block individually, keeping them organized by block to simplify the piecing steps.

From *each* of the 6 red charm squares, cut:

1 rectangle, 2⅞" × 5" (combined total of 6); from this rectangle cut:

- ✦ 1 square, 2⅞" × 2⅞" (combined total of 6); cut in half *once* diagonally to yield 2 triangles (combined total of 12)
- ✦ 1 square, 1½" × 1½" (combined total of 6)

1 rectangle, 1½" × 5"; crosscut into 3 squares, 1½" × 1½" (combined total of 24, including previously cut squares)

From *each* of 6 medium or dark prints, cut one set of A pieces consisting of:

1 square, 1⅞" × 1⅞" (combined total of 6); cut in half diagonally *once* to yield 2 triangles (combined total of 12)

1 rectangle, 1½" × 2½" (combined total of 6)

For *each* A set, select a different medium or dark print and cut one set of B pieces consisting of:

1 square, 1⅞" × 1⅞" (combined total of 6); cut in half diagonally *once* to yield 2 triangles (combined total of 12)

1 rectangle, 1½" × 2½" (combined total of 6)

1 square, 1½" × 1½" (combined total of 6)

From the remainder of the assorted medium and dark print scraps, cut a *combined total* of:

6 rectangles, 1" × 7½"

12 rectangles, 1" × 6½"

12 rectangles, 1" × 5½"

6 rectangles, 1" × 4½"

From *each* of the 6 assorted cream prints, cut:

1 square, 2⅞" × 2⅞" (combined total of 6); cut in half diagonally *once* to yield 2 triangles (combined total of 12)

1 square, 1⅞" × 1⅞" (combined total of 6); cut in half diagonally *once* to yield 2 triangles (combined total of 12)

2 rectangles, 1½" × 2½" (combined total of 12)

5 squares, 1½" × 1½" (combined total of 30)

From the remainder of the assorted cream prints, cut a *combined total* of:*

6 rectangles, 1" × 7½"

12 rectangles, 1" × 6½"

12 rectangles, 1" × 5½"

6 rectangles, 1" × 4½"

*For a super scrappy look, I cut a handful of rectangles from additional cream prints in my stash. This option is entirely up to you!

From the gold print, cut:

2 strips, 1" × 21½"

2 strips, 1" × 15½"

From the black print, cut:

2 strips, 2½" × 42"; crosscut into 2 strips, 2½" × 22½", for border #2. Set aside the remainder of both strips for the binding.*

3 additional binding strips, 2½" × 42"*

*For my chubby-binding method on page 111, reduce the strip width to 2".

From the plum print, cut:

2 strips, 2½" × 24½"

From the brown print, cut:

2 strips, 2½" × 23½"

Piecing the Blocks

Sew all pieces with right sides together using a ¼" seam allowance unless otherwise noted. Press the seam allowances as indicated by the arrows.

1 Select one set of pieces cut from a single red print, one set of A pieces cut from a single medium or dark print, and one set of B pieces cut from a different medium or dark print. From the assorted cream prints, randomly select:

- ◆ 1 triangle cut from a 2⅞" square
- ◆ 2 triangles cut from 1⅞" squares
- ◆ 2 rectangles, 1½" × 2½"
- ◆ 5 squares, 1½" × 1½"

2 Join a cream and a red 2⅞" triangle along the long diagonal edges. Press. Trim away the dog-ear points for a large half-square-triangle unit measuring 2½" square, including the seam allowances. Repeat using the two cream 1⅞" triangles and the two medium or dark 1⅞" triangles from the A and B sets to piece two small half-square-triangle units measuring 1½" square, including the seam allowances. You'll have one leftover red 2⅞" triangle and two leftover 1⅞" medium or dark triangles.

Make 1
red unit,
2½" × 2½".

Make 1 each
of A and B,
1½" × 1½".

3 Use a pencil and an acrylic ruler to draw a diagonal sewing line from corner to corner on the wrong side of the red 1½" squares and four of the assorted cream 1½" squares.

4 Layer a prepared cream 1½" square onto one end of each A and B 1½" × 2½" rectangle as shown. Stitch along the drawn lines. Press. Trim away the layers beneath the resulting top cream triangles, leaving a ¼" seam allowance. In the same manner, add a mirror-image cream star point to each rectangle. The pieced star-point units should measure 1½" × 2½", including the seam allowances.

Make 1 each of A and B,
1½" × 2½".

5 Referring to step 4, use the four prepared red 1½" squares and two cream 1½" × 2½" rectangles to piece two red star-point units measuring 1½" × 2½", including the seam allowances.

Make 2 red units,
1½" × 2½".

Finished quilt size: 23½" × 30½"
Finished block size: 7" × 7"

DESIGNED AND PIECED BY *Kim Diehl*
MACHINE QUILTED BY *Rebecca Silbaugh*

6 Lay out the large and small half-square-triangle units from step 2, the A and B star-point units from step 4, the two red star-point units from step 5, and the remaining cream and medium or dark 1½" squares in three horizontal rows to form the patchwork star. Join the pieces in each row. Press. Join the rows. Press. The pieced star unit should measure 4½" square, including the seam allowances.

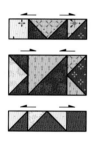

Star unit,
4½" × 4½"

7 Repeat steps 1–6 to piece a total of six star units.

8 Join a cream and a medium or dark 1" × 4½" rectangle to opposite sides of a star unit, sewing the cream strip to the cream edge and the dark strip to the dark edge as shown. Press. Join a cream and a medium or dark 1" × 5½" rectangle to the top and bottom of the star unit as shown. Press.

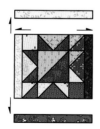

9 Continue adding cream and medium or dark rectangles to opposite sides of the star unit as shown to build the block. Press all seam allowances away from the star unit except for the final light strip. Press it toward the block center so that the seam allowances will abut when assembling the quilt top. The pieced patchwork block should measure 7½" square, including the seam allowances.

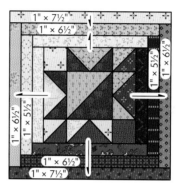

Patchwork block,
7½" × 7½"

10 Repeat steps 8 and 9 to piece a total of six patchwork blocks.

Piecing the Quilt Center

1 Referring to the quilt assembly diagram on page 18, lay out the six patchwork blocks in three horizontal rows, rotating the blocks as needed to form the diagonal patchwork pattern.

2 Join the blocks in each row. Press the seam allowances open. Join the rows. Press the seam allowances open. The pieced quilt center should measure 14½" × 21½", including the seam allowances.

Adding the Borders

1 Join the gold 1" × 21½" strips to the right and left sides of the quilt center. Press seam allowances toward the gold strips. Join the gold 1" × 15½" strips to the top and bottom of the quilt center. Press seam allowances toward the gold strips.

2 Add the black 2½" × 22½" strips to the right and left sides of the quilt center. Press. Join the teal 1½" × 19½" strips to the top and bottom of the quilt center. Press.

3 Sew the plum 2½" × 24½" strips to the right and left sides of the quilt center. Press. Join the burnt-orange 1½" × 23½" strips to the top and bottom of the quilt center. Press.

4 Join the brown 2½" × 23½" strips to the top and bottom of the quilt center. Press.

Completing the Quilt

Layer and baste the quilt top, batting, and backing. Quilt the layers. The featured quilt was machine quilted with straight lines echoing out from the star centers to form Vs that extend into the star points. The dark courthouse steps strips were stitched with a 1" diagonal crosshatch design, with meandering feathered fronds on the light strips. The border strips feature a variety of motifs, with the chosen designs mirrored on each opposite side of the quilt for balance. Referring to "Chubby Binding" on page 111, or substituting your own favorite method, use black binding strips to bind the quilt.

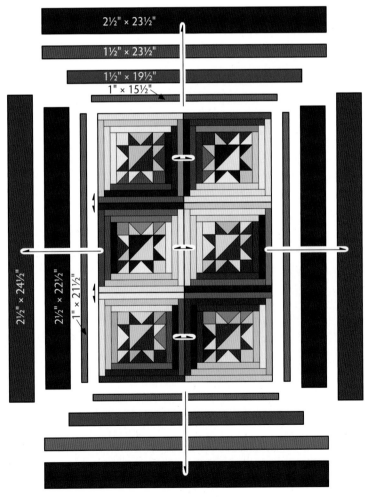

2½" × 23½"

1½" × 23½"

1½" × 19½"
1" × 15½"

2½" × 24½"

2½" × 22½"

1" × 21½"

Quilt assembly

Crackers and Marmalade

BEDROOM ENSEMBLE

*V*ivid and bold is also classic, timeless, and refined in this pieced houndstooth-inspired quilt that only *looks* complicated—you'll find it's a snap to stitch! Add enticing layers of coordinating textures with easily pieced pillowcases and a patchwork throw pillow, and your bed will be dressed to the nines.

 Bed Quilt

FINISHED QUILT SIZE: 72½" × 88½"

FINISHED BLOCK SIZE: 8" × 8"

Materials

Yardage is based on 42" of usable fabric width after prewashing and removing selvages. For greater ease and versatility, materials and instructions for the Star Blossom Throw Pillow are provided separately, beginning on page 24.

- ✦ 5¼ yards of cheddar print for patchwork and binding
- ✦ 4⅛ yards of cream print for patchwork
- ✦ 6¾ yards of fabric for backing
- ✦ 81" × 97" rectangle of batting

To find free downloadable instructions for the patchwork pillowcase online, visit tinyurl.com/11588-patterns-download

Cutting

Cut all pieces across the width of the fabric in the order given unless otherwise noted.

From the cheddar print, cut:

6 strips, 8⅞" × 42"; crosscut *each* strip into 4 squares, 8⅞" × 8⅞" (total of 24). Cut each square in half diagonally *once* to yield 2 triangles (total of 48).

1 strip, 8⅞" × 42"; crosscut into:
- ✦ 1 square, 8⅞" × 8⅞". Cut in half diagonally *once* to yield 2 triangles (combined total of 50, including the previously cut triangles).
- ✦ 6 squares, 4½" × 4½"

7 strips, 8½" × 42"; crosscut *each* strip into 4 squares, 8½" × 8½" (total of 28). From the remainder of each strip, cut 1 square, 4½" × 4½" (combined total of 13, including the previously cut squares).

1 strip, 8½" × 42"; crosscut into 2 squares, 8½" × 8½" (combined total of 30, including the previously cut squares). From the remainder of the strip, cut 4 squares, 4½" × 4½" (combined total of 17, including the previously cut squares).

4 strips, 4½" × 42"; crosscut into 32 squares, 4½" × 4½" (combined total of 49, including the previously cut squares)

9 binding strips, 2½" × 42" (for my chubby-binding method on page 111, reduce the strip width to 2")

From the cream print, cut:

7 strips, 8⅞" × 42"; crosscut into 25 squares, 8⅞" × 8⅞". Cut each square in half diagonally *once* to yield 2 triangles (total of 50).

5 strips, 8½" × 42"; crosscut *each* strip into 4 squares, 8½" × 8½" (total of 20). From the remainder of each strip, cut 1 square, 4½" × 4½" (total of 5).

6 strips, 4½" × 42"; crosscut into 44 squares, 4½" × 4½" (combined total of 49, including the previously cut squares)

Piecing the Blocks

Sew all pieces with right sides together using a ¼" seam allowance unless otherwise noted. Press the seam allowances as indicated by the arrows.

1 Layer and stitch a cream and a cheddar 8⅞" triangle along the long diagonal edges. Press. Trim away the dog-ear points. Repeat to piece a total of 49 half-square-triangle units measuring 8½" square, including the seam allowances. You'll have one leftover cream triangle and one leftover cheddar triangle.

 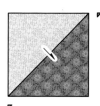

Make 49 units,
8½" × 8½".

2 Use a pencil and an acrylic ruler to draw a diagonal sewing line from corner to corner on the wrong side of each cream and cheddar 4½" square.

3 Referring to the illustration on page 23, layer a prepared cream square on one corner of a step 1 half-square-triangle unit and a prepared cheddar square on the opposite corner. Stitch the squares along the drawn lines. Fold each resulting inner triangle open, aligning the corner with the corner of the half-square-triangle unit. Press. Trim away the

Finished quilt size: 72½" × 88½"
Finished block size: 8" × 8"

DESIGNED AND PIECED BY *Kim Diehl*
MACHINE QUILTED BY *Connie Tabor*

layers beneath the top triangles, leaving ¼" seam allowances. Repeat to piece a total of 49 blocks measuring 8½" square, including the seam allowances.

 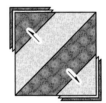

Make 49 blocks,
8½" × 8½".

Piecing the Quilt Top

1 Lay out five cheddar 8½" squares and four blocks in alternating positions as shown. Join the pieces. Press. Repeat to piece a total of six A rows measuring 8½" × 72½", including the seam allowances.

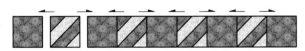

Make 6 A rows, 8½" × 72½".

2 Rotating the blocks to achieve the color placement shown, lay out five blocks and four cream 8½" squares in alternating positions. Join the pieces. Press. Repeat to piece a total of five B rows measuring 8½" × 72½", including the seam allowances.

Make 5 B rows, 8½" × 72½".

3 Referring to the quilt assembly diagram below, lay out the A and B rows in alternating positions. Join the rows. Press.

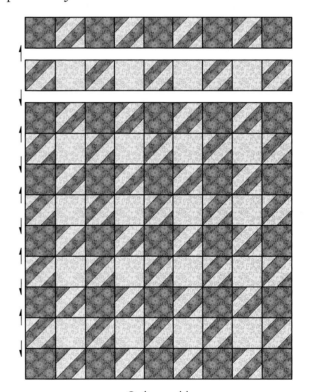

Quilt assembly

Completing the Quilt

Layer and baste the quilt top, batting, and backing. Quilt the layers. The featured quilt was machine quilted with an edge-to-edge orange peel design. Referring to "Chubby Binding" on page 111, or substituting your own favorite method, use the cheddar binding strips to bind the quilt.

Crackers and Marmalade Bedroom Ensemble

Star Blossom Throw Pillow

FINISHED THROW PILLOW SIZE: 14½" × 14½"

Materials

Yardage is based on 42" of usable fabric width after prewashing and removing selvages.

+ ½ yard of cream print for patchwork and pillow back
+ ½ yard of cheddar print for patchwork and binding
+ 18" × 18" square of bleached muslin for pillow front lining
+ 18" × 18" square of batting
+ Liquid seam sealant, such as Fray Check
+ 14" × 14" pillow form

Cutting

From the cream print, cut:
1 strip, 14½" × 42"; crosscut into 2 rectangles, 11¼" × 14½". From the remainder of this strip, cut:
+ 1 square, 3½" × 3½"
+ 4 rectangles, 2" × 3½"
+ 6 squares, 2⅜" × 2⅜"; cut each square in half diagonally *once* to yield 2 triangles (total of 12)
+ 16 squares, 2" × 2"

From the cheddar print, cut:
1 strip, 3½" × 42"; crosscut into 4 squares, 3½" × 3½". From the remainder of the strip, cut 6 squares, 2⅜" × 2⅜"; cut each square in half diagonally *once* to yield 2 triangles (total of 12).
2 strips, 2" × 42"; crosscut into:
+ 8 rectangles, 2" × 3½"
+ 8 squares, 2" × 2"
+ 2 rectangles, 1½" × 12½"
3 strips, 1½" × 42"; crosscut *1 of the strips* into 2 rectangles, 1½" × 14½". Reserve the remaining 2 strips for the binding.

Piecing the Pillow Front

Sew all pieces with right sides together using a ¼" seam allowance unless otherwise noted. Press the seam allowances as indicated by the arrows or otherwise instructed.

1 Use a pencil and an acrylic ruler to draw a diagonal sewing line from corner to corner on the wrong side of the cream 2" squares.

2 Layer a prepared cream square onto one end of a cheddar 2" × 3½" rectangle. Stitch the pair together along the drawn line. Fold the resulting inner triangle open, aligning the corner with the corner of the rectangle. Press. Trim away the layers beneath the top triangle, leaving a ¼" seam allowance. In the same manner, use a second prepared cream square to add a mirror-image star point on the remaining end of the cheddar rectangle. Repeat to piece a total of eight star-point units measuring 2" × 3½", including the seam allowances.

Make 8 units, 2" × 3½".

3 Join a cream and a cheddar 2⅜" triangle along the long diagonal edges. Press. Trim away the dog-ear points. Repeat to piece a total of 12 half-square-triangle units measuring 2" square, including the seam allowances.

Make 12 units, 2" × 2".

4 Lay out a cream 3½" square, four star-point units, and four half-square-triangle units in three horizontal rows as shown on page 26. Join the

pieces in each row. Press. Join the rows. Press. The pieced center star unit should measure 6½" square, including the seam allowances.

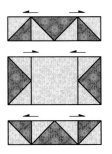
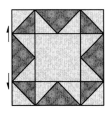

Make 1 center unit, 6½" × 6½".

5 Lay out two cheddar 2" squares, one star-point unit, two half-square-triangle units, and one cream 2" × 3½" rectangle in two horizontal rows as shown. Join the pieces in each row. Press. Join the rows. Press. Repeat to piece a total of four half-star units measuring 3½" × 6½", including the seam allowances.

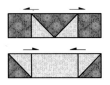

Make 4 half-star units, 3½" × 6½".

6 Lay out the center star unit, the half-star units, and four cheddar 3½" squares in three

horizontal rows. Join the pieces in each row. Press. Join the rows. Press. The pieced star unit should measure 12½" square, including the seam allowances.

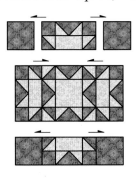
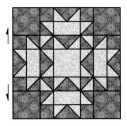

Make 1 Star unit, 12½" × 12½".

7 Join a cheddar 1½" × 12½" rectangle to the right and left sides of the star unit. Press. Join the cheddar 1½" × 14½" rectangles to the remaining sides of the star unit to complete the pillow front. Press.

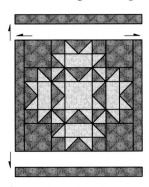

Make 1 pillow front, 14½" × 14½".

Piecing the Pillow Back

1 Apply liquid seam sealant to one 14½" edge of each cream 11¼" × 14½" rectangle.

2 Fold the long prepared edge over 2", wrong sides together; press the fold. Repeat with the remaining cream rectangle.

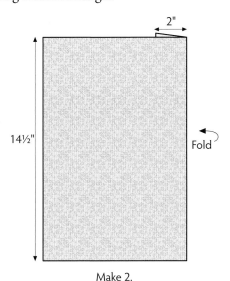

2"

14½"

Fold

Make 2.

3 Lay out the pressed cream rectangles right side up, overlapping the folded edges to make a 14½" square. Pin the overlapped sections. Machine stitch the overlapped edges using a ⅛" seam allowance to complete the pillow back.

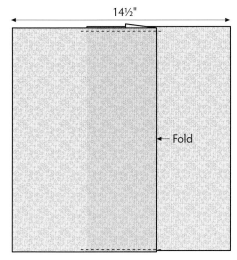

14½"

Fold

Stitch overlapped edges,
⅛" from top and bottom edges.

Completing the Throw Pillow

1 Layer and baste the pillow front, batting, and muslin lining. Quilt the layers. The featured throw pillow is machine quilted with an edge-to-edge orange peel design. Trim away the excess batting and lining, leaving a 14½"-square pillow top.

2 Layer the quilted pillow top and back wrong sides together; pin the edges well. Use a ⅛" seam allowance to sew around the perimeter of the pinned unit, joining the front and back pieces to prepare them for the binding step.

3 Join the cheddar 1½" × 42" lengths to make one long strip; press the seam allowances open. Lay the strip on your pressing surface, wrong side up. Working your way along the strip, fold the long side edges to the center, pressing them in place as you go. Referring to "Chubby Binding" on page 111, use the pressed cheddar strip and a ¼" seam allowance to bind the throw pillow. Insert the pillow form through the opening in the back, and fluff your pillow!

Crackers and Marmalade Bedroom Ensemble   **27**

Woven
TABLE TOPPER

Nine Patches are so dang cute and so much fun to stitch, they're often one of the very first blocks we tackle as we're learning to sew quilts. These little gems are super simple to piece, can be used in an endless number of ways, and the quilts they're sewn into are fantastically easy to live with.

- - - - - - -

FINISHED QUILT SIZE
40½" × 40½"

FINISHED BLOCK SIZE
8" × 8"

Materials

Yardage is based on 42" of usable fabric width after prewashing and removing selvages.

- ✦ 1 fat quarter (18" × 21") of cream print #1 for patchwork
- ✦ 1 fat quarter of cream print #2 for patchwork
- ✦ 25 chubby sixteenths (9" × 10½") of assorted prints for patchwork
- ✦ ½ yard of black print for binding
- ✦ 2⅝ yards of fabric for backing
- ✦ 47" × 47" square of batting

Cutting

Cut all pieces across the width of the fabric in the order given unless otherwise noted.

From cream print #1, cut:
52 squares, 2¼" × 2¼"

From cream print #2, cut:
48 squares, 2¼" × 2¼"

Continued on page 30

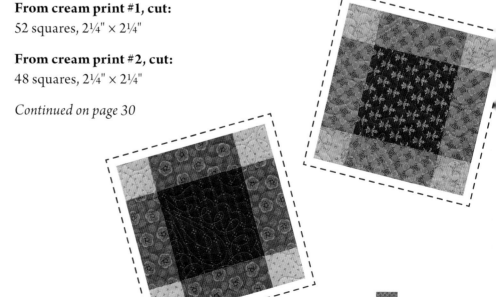

Continued from page 29

From *each* of the 25 assorted print chubby sixteenths, cut:

1 rectangle, 5" × 10½"; crosscut into:

+ 1 square, 5" × 5" (combined total of 25)
+ 2 rectangles, 2¼" × 5" (combined total of 50)

1 rectangle, 2¼" × 10½"; crosscut into 2 rectangles, 2¼" × 5" (grand total of 100, including the previously cut rectangles)

Place the 5" squares into one stack; keep the remaining rectangles organized by print.

From the black print, cut:

5 binding strips, 2½" × 42" (for my chubby-binding method provided on page 111, reduce the strip width to 2")

Piecing the Nine Patch Variation Blocks

Sew all pieces with right sides together using a ¼" seam allowance unless otherwise noted. Press the seam allowances as indicated by the arrows.

1 Select one set of 2¼" × 5" rectangles cut from a single print, one 5" square cut from a complementary print, and four 2¼" cream print #1 squares. Lay out the pieces in three horizontal rows as shown. Join the pieces in each row. Press. Join the rows. Press. Repeat to piece a total of 13 Nine Patch Variation A blocks measuring 8½" square, including the seam allowances.

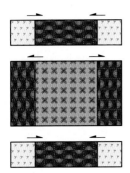
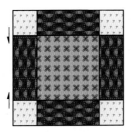

Make 13 A blocks,
8½" × 8½".

2 Repeat step 1 to piece 12 Nine Patch Variation B blocks, substituting cream print #2 and adjusting the direction of the pressed seam allowances as shown.

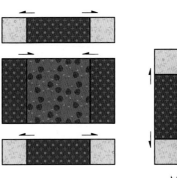
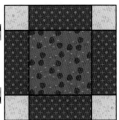

Make 12 B blocks,
8½" × 8½".

Piecing the Quilt Top

1 Lay out three A blocks and two B blocks in alternating positions. Join the blocks. Press. Repeat to piece a total of three #1 rows measuring 8½" × 40½", including seam allowances.

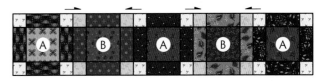

Make 3 of row #1, 8½" × 40½".

2 Lay out three B blocks and two A blocks in alternating positions. Join the blocks. Press. Repeat to piece a total of two #2 rows measuring 8½" × 40½", including the seam allowances.

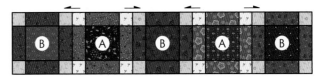

Make 2 of row #2, 8½" × 40½".

Finished quilt size: 40½" × 40½"
Finished block size: 8" × 8"

DESIGNED BY *Kim Diehl*
PIECED BY *Connie Tabor* AND *Kim Diehl*
MACHINE QUILTED BY *Connie Tabor*

3 Referring to the quilt assembly diagram below, lay out rows #1 and #2 in alternating positions. Join the rows. Press.

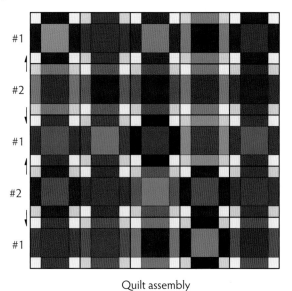

#1
#2
#1
#2
#1

Quilt assembly

pin point

Embracing Your Curves: With all of the squares and rectangles pieced into this quilt, choosing a quilting design with gently curved flowing lines is a perfect way to soften the look of the patchwork and achieve a beautiful sense of balance.

Completing the Quilt

Layer and baste the quilt top, batting, and backing. Quilt the layers. The featured quilt was machine quilted with a large-scale edge-to-edge design of stylized paisley shapes. Referring to "Chubby Binding" on page 111, or substituting your own favorite method, use the black binding strips to bind the quilt.

Prairie Moon

ENSEMBLE

 Lap Quilt

- -

Finished quilt size: 60½" × 60½"

Finished block size: 8" × 8"

- -

Materials

Yardage is based on 42" of usable fabric width after prewashing and removing selvages. Materials for the bonus projects are provided separately and begin on page 41.

- ✦ 1⅓ yards of navy print for patchwork, inner and outer borders, and binding
- ✦ 17 fat quarters (18" × 21") of assorted prints for patchwork
- ✦ ½ yard *each* of 6 assorted cream prints for patchwork
- ✦ 3¾ yards of fabric for backing
- ✦ 67" × 67" square of batting

Large-scale Snowball blocks are fun and fast to stitch, and a zigzag border is the perfect finishing touch. Best of all, this quilt includes an unexpected nice surprise—you can save and repurpose your trimmed patchwork scraps into two sweet bonus projects!

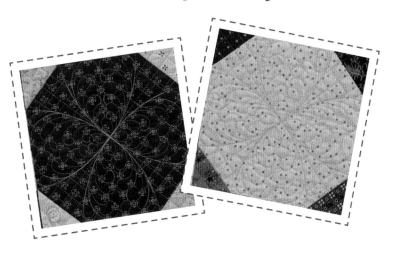

Cutting

Cut all pieces across the width of the fabric in the order given unless otherwise noted.

From the navy print, cut:

1 strip, 8½" × 42"; crosscut into 1 square, 8½" × 8½". From the remainder of the strip, cut:
- 4 squares, 2½" × 2½"
- 3 strips, 1½" × 30"

10 strips, 1½" × 42". Crosscut *1 of the strips* into 8 rectangles, 1½" × 4½". Reserve the remainder of the strips.

7 binding strips, 2½" × 42" (for my chubby-binding method on page 111, reduce the strip width to 2")

From *each* of the 17 assorted print fat quarters, cut:

1 square, 8½" × 8½" (combined total of 17)
4 squares, 2½" × 2½" (combined total of 68)
Reserve the remainder of the assorted prints.

From the reserved remainder of the assorted prints, cut a *combined total* of:

48 pairs of matching squares, 3½" × 3½" (total of 96 squares). Keep the squares organized by print.
4 squares, 4½" × 4½" (middle border corners)

From *each* of the 6 assorted cream prints, cut:

1 strip, 8½" × 42"; crosscut into 3 squares, 8½" × 8½" (combined total of 18). From the remainder of the strip, cut 12 squares, 2½" × 2½" (combined total of 72).
1 strip, 4½" × 42"; crosscut into 8 squares, 4½" × 4½" (combined total of 48)

From *each of 4* assorted cream prints, cut:

1 square, 1½" × 1½" (combined total of 4)

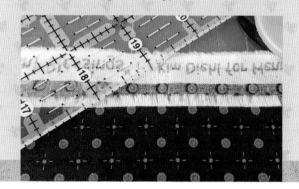
Piecing the Snowball Blocks

Sew all pieces with right sides together using a ¼" seam allowance unless otherwise noted. Press the seam allowances as indicated by the arrows or otherwise instructed.

1 Use a pencil and an acrylic ruler to draw a diagonal sewing line from corner to corner on the wrong side of each navy, cream, and assorted print 2½" square. Repeat with the assorted print 3½" squares. Reserve the prepared 3½" squares for later use.

Finished quilt size: 60½" × 60½"
Finished block size: 8" × 8"

 DESIGNED AND PIECED BY *Kim Diehl*
MACHINE QUILTED BY *Rebecca Silbaugh*

2 Choose four prepared assorted cream 2½" squares. Layer a cream square onto one corner of the navy 8½" square. Stitch the pair together along the drawn line. Fold the resulting inner triangle open, aligning the corner with the corner of the navy square. Press. Trim away the layers beneath the top triangle, leaving a ¼" seam allowance. In the same manner, stitch cream squares to the remaining corners of the navy square to complete a Snowball block. Repeat using the assorted print 8½" squares and the remaining cream 2½" squares to piece a total of 18 dark Snowball blocks measuring 8½" square, including the seam allowances.

Make 18 dark
Snowball blocks,
8½" × 8½".

3 Using the cream 8½" squares and the prepared navy and assorted print 2½" squares, repeat step 2 to piece a total of 18 light Snowball blocks measuring 8½" square, including the seam allowances.

Make 18 light Snowball blocks,
8½" × 8½".

Piecing the Quilt Center

1 Referring to the quilt-center assembly diagram at right, lay out three dark Snowball blocks and three light Snowball blocks in alternating positions. Join the blocks. Press. Repeat to piece a total of six block rows measuring 8½" × 48½", including the seam allowances.

2 Using the diagram as a guide and turning the direction of every other row, lay out the six block rows to form the quilt center. Join the rows; press. The pieced quilt center should measure 48½" square, including the seam allowances.

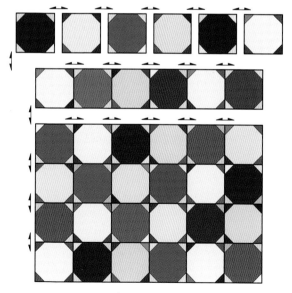

Quilt-center assembly

Creating Bonus Half-Square-Triangle Units:
*The stitch-and-fold triangle technique used in this
project results in excess layers beneath the top sewn
triangles, which are generally trimmed away and
discarded. For larger-scale corner triangles like
those featured in the border of this project, adding
a couple of quick steps gives you the option of
saving and repurposing these scraps, eliminating
waste. Here's a summary of the steps I use:*

1 In step 1 of "Piecing and Adding the Middle
Border" (page 39), after stitching the smaller
top square to the bottom square along the drawn
diagonal line, *before* pressing or trimming the
stitched triangle open, use a pencil and an acrylic
ruler to draw a second diagonal line ½" out from
the previously sewn seam. Stitch the pair together
along the newly drawn line.

2 Next, *before trimming away the stitched corner
layers,* fold the original inner triangle open,
aligning the corner with the corner of the bottom
square. Press. (Keeping the bottom layers in place
for this pressing step will help align the corner
triangle edges properly, eliminating the need to
square up the unit.) Flip the pressed top triangle
back to once again expose the layers underneath.
Cut through the layers between the two diagonal
seamlines as shown, leaving ¼" seam allowances
along each line of stitching.

3 Press the resulting bonus half-square-
triangle unit open, with the seam
allowances directed toward the darker print.

Save these half-square-triangle units as is,
trimming them to the needed size when you're
ready to repurpose them into a bonus project.

Simple Patchwork

Piecing and Adding the Inner Border

1 Join the navy 1½" × 30" and 1½" × 42" strips end to end to make one long length. Press the seam allowances open. From this pieced length, cut four 1½" × 48½" strips, two 1½" × 58½" strips, and two 1½" × 60½" strips.

2 Join a navy 1½" × 48½" strip to the right and left sides of the quilt center. Press the seam allowances toward the navy strips. Join a cream 1½" square to each end of the remaining two navy 1½" × 48½" strips. Press the seam allowances toward the navy strips. Join these pieced strips to the remaining sides of the quilt center. Press the seam allowances toward the navy strips. The quilt should measure 50½" square, including seam allowances. Reserve the remaining strips from step 1 for later use.

Piecing and Adding the Middle Border

1 Select one cream 4½" square and two prepared 3½" squares cut from a single matching print. Use the prepared squares to stitch a triangle onto two opposite corners of the cream 4½" square as previously instructed in step 2 of "Piecing the Snowball Blocks" on page 37. *If you plan to make one or both of the bonus projects beginning on page 41, please refer to the Pin Point tip on page 38 for instructions on trimming and completing the unit.* To complete the border blocks for this project without repurposing the patchwork scraps, finish the unit as described in the referenced step 2. Repeat to piece a total of 48 border units measuring 4½" square, including the seam allowances.

Make 48 units,
4½" × 4½".

2 Join the border units in pairs as shown to make 24 units, 4½" × 8½", including the seam allowances. Press the seam allowances to one side, in the direction that produces the best points.

Make 24 border units,
4½" × 8½".

3 Join six border units end to end. Press the seam allowances to one side, in the direction that will produce the best points. Repeat to piece a total of four border strips measuring 4½" × 48½", including the seam allowances. Join a navy 1½" × 4½" rectangle to each end of the border strips. Press the seam allowances toward the navy rectangles. The completed middle border strips should measure 4½" × 50½", including the seam allowances.

Make 4 borders, 4½" × 50½".

4 Join a pieced middle border strip to the right and left sides of the quilt top, referring to the borders diagram on page 40 for the correct orientation. Press the seam allowances toward the inner border. Join an assorted print 4½" square to each end of the remaining two pieced border strips. Press the seam allowances toward the navy rectangles. Join these border strips to the remaining sides of the quilt top. Press the seam allowances toward the inner border. The quilt top should now measure 58½" square, including the seam allowances.

Pinning Patchwork: For accurate patchwork seams and intersections, especially when joining units with diagonal seams, I'm a firm believer in pinning. To help me achieve good results for the zigzag border units in this quilt, I layered the blocks right sides together, and then pinched them firmly between my thumb and fingers at the position where the diagonal cream seams met. While continuing to pinch the pieces together, I used my other hand to fold open the fabric edges at the point I was pinching to ensure the seams were perfectly aligned; for any that were a bit off, I tweaked the placement. Once I was pleased with the fit, I pinned the layers in place (taking care not to shift them) and checked the result one last time to ensure nothing had moved out of alignment. I worked from that pinned position outward to each opposite edge to complete the pinning. If there was a slight difference at the unit edges after matching up the diagonal cream seams, I didn't let this worry me, because I knew they would be absorbed into the seam allowances when the pieced unit was joined to the quilt top. Pinning the units at the seams that are the focal point first, and then working outward, is a great way to achieve accuracy.

Adding the Outer Border

Join the navy 1½" × 58½" strips to the right and left sides of the quilt top; press. Join the navy 1½" × 60½" strips to the remaining sides of the quilt top. Press.

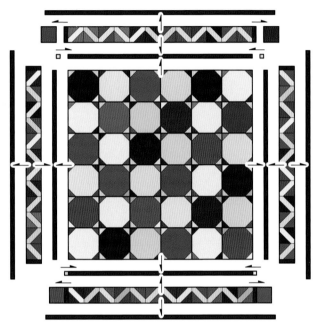

Adding borders

Completing the Quilt

Layer and baste the quilt top, batting, and backing. Quilt the layers. The featured quilt was machine quilted with an orange peel design radiating out from the center of each Snowball block, and each orange peel shape was filled with feathers; the block corners and open spaces between the orange peels were stitched with a diagonal crosshatch. The dark triangles of the middle border were stitched with a dahlia design, with repeating straight lines stitched within the cream zigzag patchwork. Referring to "Chubby Binding" on page 111, or substituting your own favorite method, use the navy binding strips to bind the quilt.

Zigging and Zagging Pillow

FINISHED PILLOW SIZE: 16½" × 16½"

Materials

Yardage is based on 42" of usable fabric width after prewashing and removing selvages.

- ✦ 64 half-square-triangle units saved from the Prairie Moon Lap Quilt*
- ✦ 1 fat eighth (9" × 21") of print for binding (I chose navy print to coordinate with the Prairie Moon quilt)
- ✦ ⅝ yard of muslin for pillow front lining
- ✦ 21" × 21" square of batting
- ✦ ⅜ yard of fabric for pillow back
- ✦ 16" × 16" pillow form
- ✦ Liquid seam sealant, such as Fray Check

* If you haven't made the Prairie Moon project, you can use 32 squares, 3" × 3", from assorted cream and dark scraps, cutting each square in half diagonally to produce two triangles, and stitching each cream triangle to a dark triangle along the long diagonal edges for 64 half-square-triangle units; these units will be trimmed to the needed size in the project steps that follow.

Cutting

From the muslin, cut:
1 square, 21" × 21"

From the fabric for the pillow back, cut:
1 strip, 12¼" × 42"; crosscut into 2 rectangles, 12¼" × 16½"

From the binding print, cut:
4 strips, 1½" × 21"

Piecing the Pillow Front

1 Align the marked diagonal line of an acrylic ruler with the seam of a half-square-triangle unit, positioning the ruler so the edges rest a small distance in from two sides of the patchwork; use a rotary cutter to trim away the fabric on these edges (this will remove the dog-ear points in the same step). Rotate the half-square-triangle unit, repositioning the ruler so the 2½" lines rest on the previously trimmed edges of the unit; trim away the remaining unit sides extending beyond the ruler to produce a 2½" half-square-triangle unit. Repeat to piece a total of 64 trimmed units.

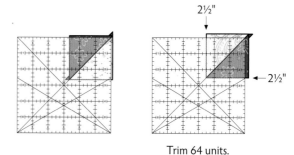

Trim 64 units.

2 Lay out the trimmed half-square-triangle units in eight horizontal rows of eight units. Or, see "Pillow Talk" on page 44 to select a different layout. When you're pleased with the placement of the prints and colors, join the units in pairs as shown. Press. The pieced pairs should measure 2½" × 4½", including the seam allowances.

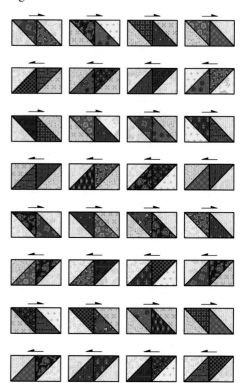

Simple Patchwork

3 Join and press the pairs to make 16 pieced V units measuring 4½" square, including the seam allowances.

Make 16 units,
4½" × 4½".

4 Join and press the V units to make four quadrants, 8½" × 8½". Join the quadrants to complete the pillow front. Press.

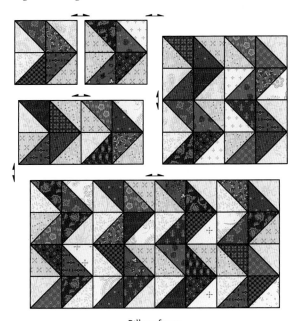

Pillow front,
16½" × 16½"

Completing the Pillow

1 Layer and baste the pillow front, batting, and muslin backing square. Quilt the layers. The featured pillow was machine quilted with repeating straight lines echoing out from the patchwork seams to create a herringbone pattern. Trim away the excess batting and backing, leaving a 16½" pillow-top square.

2 To make the pillow back, apply liquid seam sealant to one 16½" edge of each of the two 12¼" × 16½" pillow back rectangles. Fold the sealed end of one rectangle over 2", wrong sides together; press the fold. Repeat with the remaining rectangle.

3 Lay the rectangles right side up, overlapping the folded ends to produce a 16½" square. Pin the overlapped edges in place and machine stitch the overlaps ⅛" in from the top and bottom raw edges.

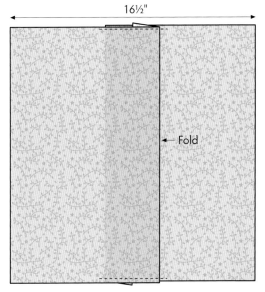

16½"

← Fold

Prairie Moon Ensemble 43

4 Layer the quilted pillow top and pillow back wrong sides together; pin the edges together. Stitch each side of the pillow unit using a ⅛" seam allowance.

5 Join the 1½"-wide binding strips end to end; press the seam allowances to one side. Position the pieced strip on your pressing surface, wrong side up. Beginning at one end, fold the outer raw edges to the center; press with a hot iron. Continue working along the strip to press the entire length. Referring to "Chubby Binding" on page 111, use the prepared strip and a ¼" seam allowance to bind the pillow. Insert the pillow form through the opening in the back.

Pillow Talk

Half-square-triangle units provide endless design opportunities because they can be arranged into countless layouts. You can use the 64 units from the project to make the featured Zigging and Zagging pillow design, or any of these four additional layouts provided to spark your creativity and give you choices!

Diamonds

Pinwheels

Stripes

Ripples

Simple Patchwork

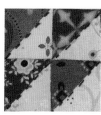

Loosey-Goosey Pincushion

FINISHED PINCUSHION SIZE: 5" × 5"

Pincushion Notes

The pincushion instructions that follow use 16 small half-square-triangle units that are trimmed to 1¼" square, as outlined in the Zigging and Zagging Pillow project on page 41, and finish at a petite ¾" square. If you're still building your patchwork skills and would like to simplify this project, you can easily substitute four larger half-square-triangle units (instead of 16) that have been trimmed to 2" square. The choice is yours!

Materials

Yardage is based on 42" of usable fabric width after prewashing and removing selvages.

- ✦ 16 half-square-triangle units saved from the Prairie Moon Lap Quilt*
- ✦ 4 rectangles, 1" × 3½", from assorted print scraps
- ✦ 4 rectangles, 1" × 5½", from assorted print scraps
- ✦ 6" × 6" square of a print of your choice for pincushion back
- ✦ 8" × 8" square of batting
- ✦ Crushed walnut shells for pincushion filling
- ✦ Fabric basting spray
- ✦ #12 perle cotton for quilting (I used Valdani's variegated Faded Brown H212)
- ✦ Size 5 embroidery needle

If you haven't made the Prairie Moon project, you can use 8 squares, 2" × 2", from assorted cream and dark scraps, cutting each square in half diagonally to produce two triangles, and stitching each cream triangle to a dark triangle along the long diagonal edges to make 16 half-square-triangle units. Working with slightly oversized triangles will make the patchwork process easier, and the units will be trimmed to the needed size in the project steps that follow.

Piecing the Pincushion

Sew all pieces with right sides together using a ¼" seam allowance. Press the seam allowances as indicated by the arrows or otherwise instructed.

1 Refer to "Piecing the Pillow Front" on page 42 to trim each half-square-triangle unit to 1¼" square, including the seam allowances. Lay out four trimmed half-square-triangle units in two horizontal rows as shown. Join the pieces in each row. Press. Join the rows. Press. Repeat to piece a total of four quarter units measuring 2" square, including the seam allowances.

Make 4 quarter units, 2" × 2".

2 Lay out the quarter units in two rows of two units each. Join the units. Press. Join the rows. Press. The pieced pincushion center unit should measure 3½" square, including the seam allowances.

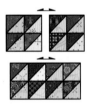

Center unit, 3½" × 3½"

3 Join two assorted print 1" × 3½" rectangles along the long edges. Press the seam allowances to one side. Repeat to piece two short rectangles. Join a short pieced rectangle to the right and left sides of the pincushion center. Press. In the same manner, join and press the assorted print

1" × 5½" rectangles to piece two long rectangles. Join these long rectangles to the top and bottom of the pincushion center. Press.

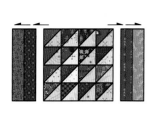
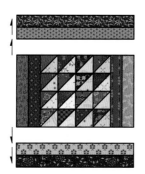

Pincushion top,
5½" × 5½"

Completing the Pincushion

1 Apply basting spray to the wrong side of the pincushion top and center it onto the batting square. (For use as a pincushion, no backing piece is needed for the quilting of this project!) Use the perle cotton and embroidery needle to sew a running stitch along the diagonal seams of the pincushion center and along the seams of the rectangles. Trim away the excess batting so the edges are flush with the pincushion top.

2 Layer the pincushion front onto the 6"-square back piece, right sides together, with the front piece centered on the larger back piece. Pin the edges. Stitch the layers together ¼" in from the pincushion-top edges, beginning and ending with several backstitches, and leaving an approximate 2" opening at the center of one side edge.

3 Trim away the excess seam allowances at each corner as shown to reduce bulk. Turn the pincushion right side out through the opening, using a skewer or pencil to push out the corners from the inside of the unit. Fill the pincushion with crushed walnut shells, turn under the unfinished edges, and use a needle and thread to hand stitch the opening closed.

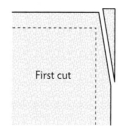

First cut

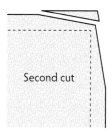

Second cut

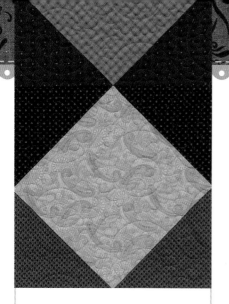

Cobblestones

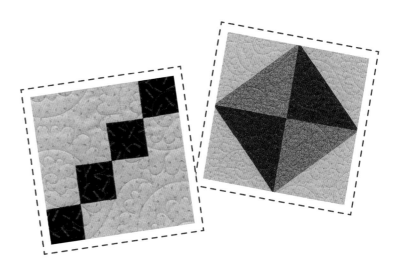

Color is everything in this easily stitched lap-sized quilt with big, chunky patchwork pieces, warm and burnished hues of autumn, and inky black "cobblestones." Rev up your sewing machine and let the ripple effect begin!

- - - - - - - -

FINISHED QUILT SIZE
64½" × 64½"

Materials

Yardage is based on 42" of usable fabric width after prewashing and removing selvages.

- ✦ 1 chubby sixteenth (9" × 10½") *each* of light and dark teal prints for patchwork
- ✦ 1⅓ yards of cream print for patchwork
- ✦ ⅝ yard *each* of gold, navy, light green, dark green, and red print for patchwork
- ✦ 1⅛ yards of tan print for patchwork
- ✦ 1 yard of black print for patchwork and binding
- ✦ 1 fat quarter (18" × 21") *each* of orange and brown prints for patchwork
- ✦ 4 yards of fabric for backing
- ✦ 71" × 71" square of batting

Cutting

Cut all pieces across the width of the fabric in the order given unless otherwise noted.

From *each* of the light and dark teal prints, cut:

1 square, 8⅞" × 8⅞" (combined total of 2); cut each square in half diagonally *once* to yield 2 triangles (combined total of 4)

From the cream print, cut:

1 strip, 8⅞" × 42"; crosscut into 2 squares, 8⅞" × 8⅞". Cut each square in half diagonally *once* to yield 2 triangles (total of 4). From the remainder of this strip, cut 8 rectangles, 2½" × 6½".

13 strips, 2½" × 42"; crosscut into:

✦ 32 rectangles, 2½" × 6½" (total of 40, including the previously cut rectangles)

✦ 40 rectangles, 2½" × 4½"

✦ 40 squares, 2½" × 2½"

From *each* of the gold, navy, dark green, and red prints, cut:

2 strips, 8½" × 42"; crosscut into 8 squares, 8½" × 8½" (combined total of 32)

From the tan print, cut:

2 strips, 16½" × 42"; crosscut into 4 squares, 16½" × 16½"

From the light green print, cut:

2 strips, 8½" × 42"; crosscut into 4 rectangles, 8½" × 16½"

From the black print, cut:

6 strips, 2½" × 42"; crosscut into 80 squares, 2½" × 2½"

7 binding strips, 2½" × 42" (for my chubby-binding method provided on page 111, reduce the strip width to 2")

From *each* of the orange and brown prints, cut:

4 squares, 8½" × 8½" (combined total of 8)

Piecing the Center Unit

Sew all pieces with right sides together using a ¼" seam allowance unless otherwise noted. Press the seam allowances as indicated by the arrows.

1 Join a dark teal and a cream 8⅞" triangle along the long diagonal edges. Press. Trim away the dog-ear points. Repeat to piece a total of two dark teal half-square-triangle units and two light teal half-square-triangle units measuring 8½" square, including the seam allowances.

Make 2 dark teal and
2 light teal units, 8½" × 8½".

2 Lay out the half-square-triangle units in two horizontal rows. Join the units in each row. Press. Join the rows. Press. The center unit should measure 16½" square, including the seam allowances.

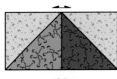
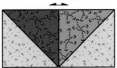
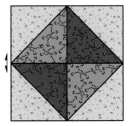

Make 1 center unit,
16½" × 16½".

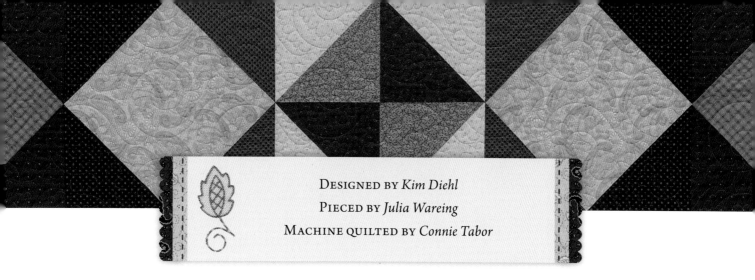

DESIGNED BY *Kim Diehl*
PIECED BY *Julia Wareing*
MACHINE QUILTED BY *Connie Tabor*

Piecing the Square-in-a-Square Units

1 Use a pencil and an acrylic ruler to draw a diagonal sewing line from corner to corner on the wrong side of each gold, navy, and dark green 8½" square. Reserve the prepared dark green squares for later use.

2 Layer a prepared gold square onto one corner of a tan 16½" square as shown. Stitch the pair along the drawn line. Fold the resulting inner triangle open, aligning the corner with the corner of the tan square. Press. Trim away the layers beneath the top triangle, leaving a ¼" seam allowance. In the same manner, add a gold triangle to the adjacent corner of the tan square. Last, add two navy triangles to the remaining tan corners. Repeat to piece a total of four square-in-a-square units measuring 16½" square, including the seam allowances.

Make 4 units,
16½" × 16½".

Piecing the Flying-Geese Units

Referring to step 2 of "Piecing the Square-in-a-Square Units" at left, use the reserved dark green squares and the light green 8½" × 16½" rectangles to piece four flying-geese units measuring 8½" × 16½", including the seam allowances.

Make 4 units,
8½" × 16½".

Piecing the Irish Chain Units

1 Join a black 2½" square to one end of a cream 2½" × 6½" rectangle. Press. Repeat to piece a total of 40 outer units measuring 2½" × 8½", including the seam allowances.

Make 40 outer units,
2½" × 8½".

2 Join a cream 2½" square and a cream 2½" × 4½" rectangle to opposite sides of a black 2½" square as shown. Press. Repeat to piece a total of 40 inner units measuring 2½" × 8½", including the seam allowances.

Make 40 inner units,
2½" × 8½".

3 Join two inner units along the long edges, positioning them as shown. Press. Repeat to piece a total of 20 inner rectangle units measuring 4½" × 8½", including the seam allowances.

Make 10 of each unit,
4½" × 8½".

4 Join an outer unit to each long side of an inner rectangle unit as shown. Press. Repeat to piece a total of 20 Irish chain units measuring 8½" square, including the seam allowances.

Make 10 of each,
8½" × 8½".

Piecing the Quilt Top

1 Lay out two red 8½" squares, one orange 8½" square, and one Irish chain unit in two horizontal rows as shown. Join the pieces in each row. Press. Piece a total of two checkerboard units measuring 16½" square, including the seam allowances. In the same manner, use the remaining red and orange squares and two Irish chain units to piece two mirror-image checkerboard units measuring 16½" square, including the seam allowances.

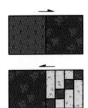

Make 2 of each unit,
16½" × 16½".

2 Lay out one checkerboard unit, four Irish chain units, and one brown 8½" square to form a corner unit. Join the Irish chain units as shown. Press. Join the brown square to the topmost Irish chain unit. Press. Join the lower Irish chain unit to the checkerboard unit. Press. Last, join the top and bottom units. Press. Repeat to piece a total of two corner units measuring 24½" square, including the seam allowances.

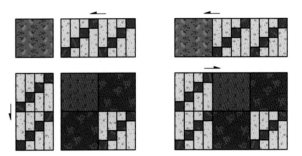

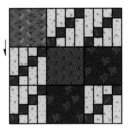

Make 2 corner units,
24½" × 24½".

3 Repeat step 2 to piece two mirror-image corner units measuring 24½" square, including the seam allowances.

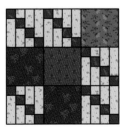

Make 2 mirror-image corner units,
24½" × 24½".

4 Join a flying-geese unit to the navy edge of a square-in-a-square unit. Press. Repeat

Simple Patchwork

to piece a total of four star-point units measuring 16½" × 24½", including the seam allowances.

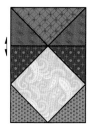

Make 4 star-point units,
16½" × 24½".

5 Referring to the quilt assembly diagram below, lay out the corner and mirror-image corner units, the star-point units, and the center unit in three horizontal rows. Join the units in each row. Press. Join the rows. Press.

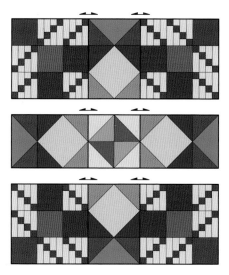

Quilt assembly

Completing the Quilt

Layer and baste the quilt top, batting, and backing. Quilt the layers. The featured quilt was machine quilted with an edge-to-edge design of large-scale curlicues, with free-form flower petals embellishing one side of the curlicue lines. Referring to "Chubby Binding" on page 111, or substituting your own favorite method, use the black binding strips to bind the quilt.

Breezy

Build your patchwork skills and enjoy some quality sewing time as you stitch the bodaciously big Pinwheel blocks featured in this fat quarter–friendly project. An array of jewel-toned prints and a breezy sense of movement make this quilt one you'll want to use again and again.

- - - - - - - -

FINISHED QUILT SIZE
62½" × 62½"

FINISHED BLOCK SIZE
10" × 10"

Materials

Yardage is based on 42" of usable fabric width after prewashing and removing selvages.

- ✦ 1⅛ yards of dark blue print for patchwork, blocks, outer border, and binding
- ✦ 17 fat quarters (18" × 21") of assorted prints for patchwork and blocks
- ✦ 1⅝ yards of cream print for patchwork
- ✦ 3⅞ yards of fabric for backing
- ✦ 69" × 69" square of batting

Cutting

Cut all pieces across the width of the fabric in the order given unless otherwise noted.

From the dark blue print, cut:
7 strips, 1½" × 42"
7 binding strips, 2½" × 42" (for my chubby-binding method provided on page 111, reduce the strip width to 2")
Reserve the remainder of the dark blue print.

From *each* of the 17 assorted prints and the reserved remainder of the dark blue print, cut:
4 squares, 5⅞" × 5⅞" (combined total of 72)
Reserve the remainder of the assorted and dark blue prints.

Continued on page 56

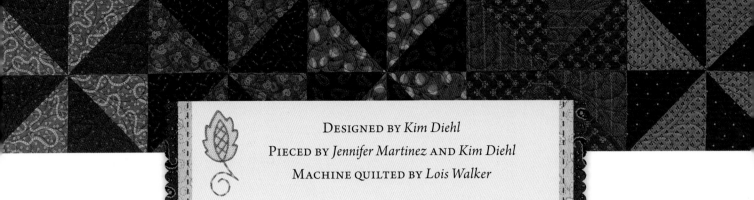

DESIGNED BY *Kim Diehl*

PIECED BY *Jennifer Martinez* AND *Kim Diehl*

MACHINE QUILTED BY *Lois Walker*

Continued from page 55

From the remainder of the dark blue and assorted prints, cut a *combined total* of:

20 squares, 5⅞" × 5⅞"; cut each square in half diagonally *once* to yield 2 triangles (combined total of 40)

16 squares, 5½" × 5½"

20 squares, 3" × 3"

From the cream print, cut;

4 strips, 5⅞" × 42"; crosscut into 20 squares, 5⅞" × 5⅞". Cut each square in half diagonally *once* to yield 2 triangles (total of 40).

4 strips, 5½" × 42"; crosscut into:

✦ 8 rectangles, 5½" × 10½"

✦ 8 squares, 5½" × 5½"

2 strips, 3" × 42"; crosscut *each* strip into:

✦ 1 strip, 3" × 15½" (total of 2)

✦ 1 strip, 3" × 20½" (total of 2)

Piecing the Pinwheel Blocks

Sew all pieces with right sides together using a ¼" seam allowance unless otherwise noted. Press the seam allowances as indicated by the arrows or otherwise instructed.

1 Choosing two complementary prints, select all four squares cut from each print for a combined total of eight. Use a pencil and an acrylic ruler to draw a diagonal line from corner to corner on the wrong side of each square of one print.

2 Layer one of the prepared squares onto a complementary print square. Sew the pair ¼" from *each* side of the drawn diagonal line. Cut the

stitched squares apart along the drawn line. Press the seam allowances of the two resulting half-square-triangle units to one side. Trim away the dog-ear points. Repeat with the remaining prepared squares to piece a total of eight identical half-square-triangle units measuring 5½" square, including the seam allowances.

Make 8 units, 5½" × 5½".

3 Lay out four matching half-square-triangle units in two horizontal rows as shown. Join the units in each row. Press. Join the rows. Press. Repeat to piece a total of two Pinwheel blocks from the pair of prints. Each block should measure 10½" square, including the seam allowances.

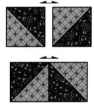

Make 2 Pinwheel blocks, 10½" × 10½".

4 Repeat steps 1–3 to piece a total of 18 Pinwheel blocks, with two blocks sewn from each pair of prints.

Piecing the Center Patchwork Unit

1 Choosing the prints randomly, lay out four assorted print 3" squares end to end. Join the

squares. Press. Repeat to piece a total of four square units measuring 3" × 10½", including the seam allowances. Sew a 3" square to each end of two of the units to make two units measuring 3" × 15½".

Make 4 units,
3" × 10½".

Make 2 units,
3" × 15½".

2 Join a 4-square unit to the right and left sides of a Pinwheel block. Press. Join a 6-square unit to the top and bottom edges of the pinwheel unit. Press. The pinwheel unit should measure 15½" square, including the seam allowances. Reserve the remaining Pinwheel blocks for later use.

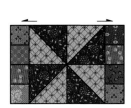

Make 1 unit,
15½" × 15½".

3 Join a cream 3" × 15½" strip to the right and left sides of the pinwheel unit. Press. Join a cream 3" × 20½" strip to the top and bottom of the pinwheel unit. Press. The center pinwheel unit should now measure 20½" square, including the seam allowances.

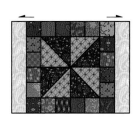
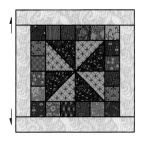

Center pinwheel unit,
20½" × 20½"

4 Draw a diagonal sewing line on the wrong side of each assorted print 5½" square as previously instructed. Layer a prepared square onto one end of a cream 5½" × 10½" rectangle as shown. Stitch the pair along the drawn line. Fold the resulting inner triangle open, aligning the corner with the corner of the rectangle. Press. Trim away the layers beneath the top triangle, leaving a ¼" seam allowance. In the same manner, add a mirror-image triangle to the remaining end of the rectangle. Repeat to piece a total of eight flying-geese units measuring 5½" × 10½", including the seam allowances.

Make 8 units, 5½" × 10½".

5 Layer a cream and a print 5⅞" triangle. Stitch the pair along the long diagonal edges. Press. Trim away the dog-ear points. Repeat to piece a total of 40 half-square-triangle units measuring 5½" square, including the seam allowances.

Make 40 units,
5½" × 5½".

6 Join a half-square-triangle unit to each side of one flying-geese unit. Press. Repeat to piece a total of four triangle rows measuring 5½" × 20½", including the seam allowances. Reserve the remaining half-square-triangle units for later use.

Make 4 triangle rows, 5½" × 20½".

7 Referring to the quilt assembly diagram below, join a triangle row to the right and left sides of the center pinwheel unit. Press. Join a cream 5½" square to each end of the remaining two triangle rows. Press. Join these rows to the top and bottom edges of the unit. Press. The pieced center patchwork unit should measure 30½" square, including the seam allowances.

Piecing and Adding the Pinwheel Border

1 Refer to the quilt assembly diagram to join three reserved Pinwheel blocks end to end. Press. Repeat to piece a total of two short pinwheel rows measuring 10½" × 30½", including the seam allowances. Join these rows to the right and left sides of the center patchwork unit. Press.

2 Using two sets of five Pinwheel blocks (one set for each row), repeat step 1 to make two long pinwheel rows measuring 10½" × 50½", including the seam allowances. You'll have one unused block left over. Join these rows to the top and bottom edges of the center patchwork unit. Press. The quilt top should measure 50½" square, including the seam allowances.

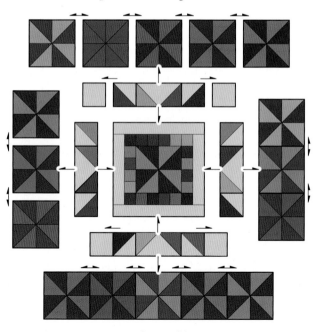

Quilt assembly

Piecing and Adding the Flying-Geese Border

1 Lay out one reserved flying-geese unit and eight reserved half-square-triangle units as shown. Join the units. Press. Repeat to piece a total of four triangle borders measuring 5½" × 50½", including the seam allowances.

Make 4 triangle borders, 5½" × 50½".

2 Refer to the borders diagram at right to join a triangle border to the right and left sides of the quilt top. Press. Join a cream 5½" square to each end of the two remaining borders. Press. Join these rows to the top and bottom edges of the quilt top. The pieced quilt top should measure 60½" square, including the seam allowances.

Adding the Outer Border

1 Join the seven dark blue 1½" × 42" strips end to end. Press the seam allowances open. From this pieced strip, cut two 60½" lengths and two 62½" lengths.

2 Join a dark blue 60½"-long strip to the right and left sides of the quilt top. Press. Join the dark blue 62½"-long strips to the top and bottom edges of the quilt top. Press.

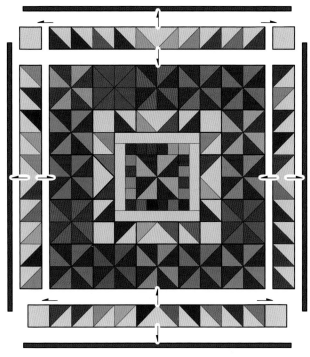

Adding borders

Completing the Quilt

Layer and baste the quilt top, batting, and backing. Quilt the layers. The featured quilt was machine quilted with an orange peel shape stitched onto each diagonal Pinwheel block seam, with feathers radiating outward to the block edge. An X was stitched onto each patchwork square, with a running feather quilted around the center pinwheel unit. The dark triangles in the outer border are stitched with repeating straight lines to echo the triangle shapes, with a free-form row of loops stitched between the center pair of lines. The cream portion of the outer border is stitched with a background fill design that randomly included pebbles, wavy lines, and paisley shapes. Referring to "Chubby Binding" on page 111, or substituting your own favorite method, use the dark blue binding strips to bind the quilt.

Evening Stroll

Simple Irish Chain and Civil War Crossing blocks alternate to bring a beautiful sense of style to this argyle-inspired quilt. Patchwork with strategically placed colors makes it difficult to tell where one block begins and the other ends, producing a design that only *looks* intricate—the piecing is a cinch! Big enough for a bed, this quilt is right at home as a table covering too.

- - - - - - -

FINISHED QUILT SIZE
70½" × 90½"

FINISHED BLOCK SIZE
10" × 10"

Materials

Yardage is based on 42" of usable fabric width after prewashing and removing selvages.

- ✦ ⅓ yard *each* of 16 assorted prints for blocks
- ✦ 2⅜ yards of black print for blocks and binding
- ✦ 1⅝ yards of cream print for blocks
- ✦ 5½ yards of fabric for backing
- ✦ 79" × 99" rectangle of batting

Cutting

Cut all pieces across the width of the fabric in the order given unless otherwise noted. To simplify the cutting steps for the 16 assorted prints, please refer to the cutting guide below.

From *each* of the 16 assorted prints, cut:
2 squares, 9¼" × 9¼" (combined total of 32); cut each
    square in half diagonally *twice* to yield 4 triangles
    (combined total of 128)
8 rectangles, 2½" × 6½" (combined total of 128)
8 squares, 2½" × 2½" (combined total of 128)
Keep the pieces organized by print.

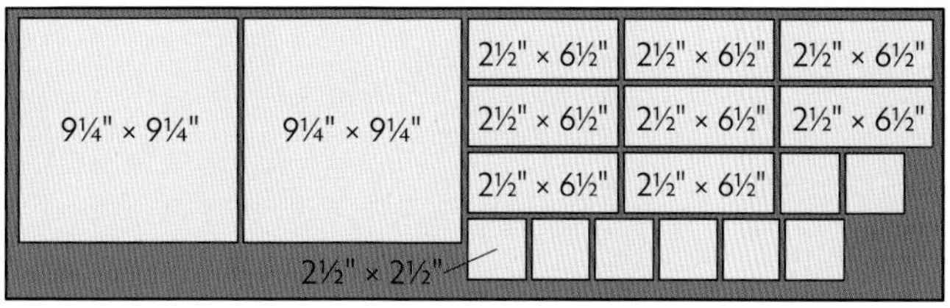

9¼" × 9¼"	9¼" × 9¼"	2½" × 6½"	2½" × 6½"	2½" × 6½"
		2½" × 6½"	2½" × 6½"	2½" × 6½"
		2½" × 6½"	2½" × 6½"	
	2½" × 2½"			

Assorted prints cutting guide

Continued on page 62

Continued from page 61

From the black print, cut:

20 strips, 2½" × 42"; crosscut into 288 squares,
2½" × 2½"

2 strips, 2" × 42"; crosscut into 31 squares, 2" × 2"

9 binding strips, 2½" × 42" (for my chubby-binding
method provided on page 111, reduce the strip
width to 2")

From the cream print, cut:

25 strips, 2" × 42"; crosscut into 124 rectangles,
2" × 7½"

Piecing the Irish Chain Blocks

Sew all pieces with right sides together using a ¼"
seam allowance unless otherwise noted. Press the seam
allowances as indicated by the arrows or otherwise
instructed.

1 Select one complete set of patchwork pieces
cut from one of the 16 assorted prints, along
with 18 black 2½" squares. Reserve the assorted print
9¼" triangles in the patchwork set for later use.

2 Lay out four matching print 2½" squares and
five black 2½" squares in three horizontal
rows as shown. Join the squares in each row. Press.
Join the rows. Press. Repeat to piece a total of two
nine-patch units measuring 6½" square, including the
seam allowances.

Make 2 nine-patch units
from each print, 6½" × 6½".

3 Join a matching print 2½" × 6½" rectangle to
opposite sides of both nine-patch units. Press.
Join a black 2½" square to each end of the remaining
four matching print 2½" × 6½" rectangles. Press. Join

these pieced rectangles to the top and bottom edges
of the nine-patch units to piece a total of two Irish
Chain blocks measuring 10½" square, including the
seam allowances. Press.

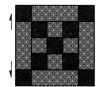

Make 2 Irish Chain blocks
from each print, 10½" × 10½".

4 Repeat steps 1–3 to piece two Irish Chain
blocks from each of the 16 assorted prints for
a combined total of 32 blocks.

Laying Out the Quilt Center

1 Use a design wall or a large floor area to lay
out the 32 Irish Chain blocks in nine rows as
shown, positioning the colors in a way that pleases you.

2 Refer to the step 3 illustration on page 64 and
use the assorted print 9¼" triangles to fill in
the open block areas between the Irish Chain blocks,
matching each print triangle to the Irish Chain block
it's resting next to. For now, leave the outermost row
of triangle spaces around the quilt perimeter open.

Finished quilt size: 70½" × 90½"
Finished block size: 10" × 10"

DESIGNED AND PIECED BY *Kim Diehl*
MACHINE QUILTED BY *Connie Tabor*

3 Use the remaining 16 triangles to fill in the final openings around the quilt-top edge. You'll have two leftover triangles.

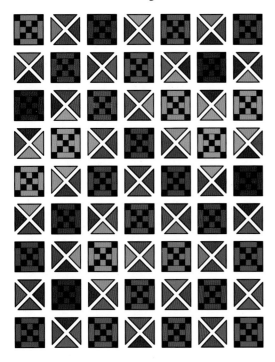

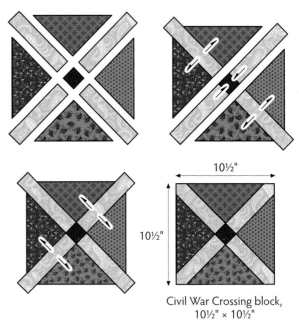

Piecing the Civil War Crossing Blocks

1 Referring to your snapped photo or swatch placement sheet to keep the print positions accurate, lay out the 9¼" triangles in the first block of the top row. In addition to the triangles, include four cream 2" × 7½" rectangles and one black 2" square as shown. Join the pieces in each diagonal row. Press. Join the rows. Press. Trim the pieced block to 10½" square, including the seam allowances, and place it back in the quilt layout.

Civil War Crossing block,
10½" × 10½"

2 Working your way across each horizontal block row, piece and reposition the Civil War Crossing blocks until the blocks in each row have been completed.

pin point

Creating a Fabric Placement Guide: *I used my digital camera to photograph the placement of the triangles in each row to help keep them in the positions I intended for the piecing steps. If you don't have a digital camera or smart phone available, another good option is to photocopy the step 3 illustration, enlarging it. Next, glue or tape small swatches of your 16 assorted prints to the photocopy, making a swatch placement sheet to document the position of your prints.*

Piecing the Quilt Top

Join the blocks in each horizontal row to piece a total of nine block rows measuring $10\frac{1}{2}" \times 70\frac{1}{2}"$, including the seam allowances. When piecing the block rows, press the seam allowances of each block toward the Irish Chain blocks. Join the rows. Press the seam allowances toward the rows that begin and end with Irish Chain blocks.

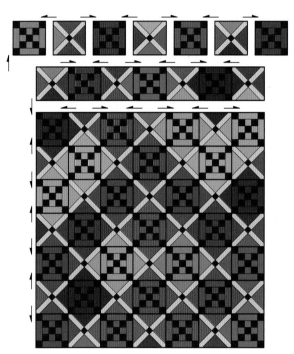

Quilt assembly

Completing the Quilt

Layer and baste the quilt top, batting, and backing. Quilt the layers. The featured quilt was machine quilted with an edge-to-edge design of repeating gentle S curves to soften the linear feel of the patchwork design. Referring to "Chubby Binding" on page 111, or substituting your own favorite method, use the black binding strips to bind the quilt.

A Dash of Plaid

With its simple shape, ease of stitching, and versatility, the modest Churn Dash block has been a favorite for generations of quilters. Embellish with a pieced buffalo-plaid center, stitch up a strippy, scrappy border, and you'll want to grab this comfy lap-sized quilt whenever you're in the mood for some serious snuggle time.

- - - - - - - -

FINISHED QUILT SIZE
62½" × 62½"

FINISHED BORDER
BLOCK SIZE
7" × 7"

Materials

Yardage is based on 42" of usable fabric width after prewashing and removing selvages. For the assorted print fat eighths, choose a blend of mostly medium and light prints, and then add a small handful of dark prints to allow the colors to stand out well from the black squares and give the illusion of buffalo plaid.

- ✦ 24 fat eighths (9" × 21") of assorted prints for patchwork
- ✦ 1¼ yards of cream print for patchwork
- ✦ ⅝ yard of black print #1 for buffalo plaid patchwork
- ✦ 1½ yards of black print #2 for Churn Dash patchwork and binding
- ✦ 3⅞ yards of fabric for backing
- ✦ 69" × 69" square of batting

Cutting

Cut all pieces across the width of the fabric in the order given unless otherwise noted.

From *each* of the 24 assorted prints, cut:
4 rectangles, 2½" × 7½" (combined total of 96)

From the remaining assorted-print scraps, cut a *combined total* of:
61 squares, 3½" × 3½"
4 squares, 3" × 3" (border corner blocks)

Continued on page 68

67

Continued from page 67

From the cream print, cut:

7 strips, 3½" × 42"; crosscut into:

- ✦ 4 strips, 3½" × 33½"
- ✦ 30 squares, 3½" × 3½"

1 strip, 3⅛" × 42"; crosscut into 8 squares, 3⅛" × 3⅛". Cut each square in half diagonally *once* to yield 2 triangles (total of 16).

2 strips, 1½" × 42"

2 squares, 8⅜" × 8⅜"; cut each square in half diagonally *once* to yield 2 triangles (total of 4)

From black print #1, cut:

3 strips, 3½" × 42"; crosscut into 30 squares, 3½" × 3½"

1 strip, 3⅛" × 42"; crosscut into 8 squares, 3⅛" × 3⅛". Cut each square in half diagonally *once* to yield 2 triangles (total of 16).

2 strips, 1¾" × 42"

From black print #2, cut:

4 strips, 5" × 33½"

2 squares, 8⅜" × 8⅜"; cut each square in half diagonally *once* to yield 2 triangles (total of 4)

7 binding strips, 2½" × 42" (for my chubby-binding method on page 111, reduce strip width to 2")

Piecing the Plaid Unit

Sew all pieces with right sides together using a ¼" seam allowance unless otherwise noted. Press the seam allowances as indicated by the arrows or otherwise instructed.

1 Lay out six assorted print 3½" squares and five cream 3½" squares in alternating positions. Join the squares. Press. Repeat to piece a total of six A rows measuring 3½" × 33½", including the seam allowances.

Make 6 A rows, 3½" × 33½".

2 Lay out five assorted print 3½" squares and six 3½" black #1 squares in alternating positions. Join the squares. Press. Repeat to piece a total of five B rows measuring 3½" × 33½", including the seam allowances.

Make 5 B rows, 3½" × 33½".

3 Lay out the A and B rows in alternating positions. Join the rows. Press. The pieced plaid unit should measure 33½" square, including the seam allowances.

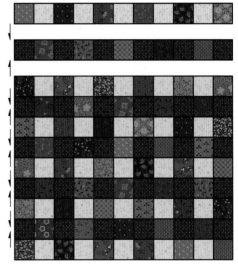

Plaid center unit, 33½" × 33½"

Piecing the Quilt Center

1 Join a cream 3½" × 33½" strip and a 5" × 33½" black #2 strip along the long edges. Press. Repeat to piece a total of four strips measuring 8" × 33½", including the seam allowances.

Make 4 strips, 8" × 33½".

Finished quilt size: 62½" × 62½"
Finished border block size: 7" × 7"

Designed by *Kim Diehl*
Pieced by *Jennifer Martinez*
Machine quilted by *Rebecca Silbaugh*

2 Layer and stitch a black #2 and a cream 8⅜" triangle along the long diagonal edges. Press. Trim away the dog-ear points. Repeat to piece a total of four half-square-triangle units measuring 8" square, including the seam allowances.

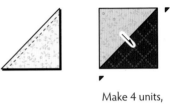

Make 4 units,
8" × 8".

3 Referring to the quilt-center assembly diagram below, lay out the pieced strips, the four half-square-triangle units, and the plaid center unit in three horizontal rows. Join the pieces in each row; press. Join the rows. Press. The pieced quilt center should measure 48½" square, including the seam allowances.

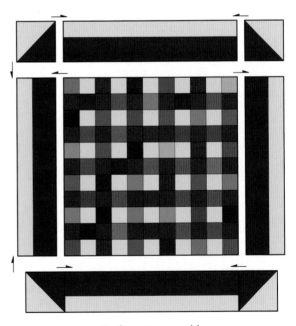

Quilt-center assembly

Piecing and Adding the Border

1 Join a cream 1½" × 42" strip and a 1¾" × 42" black #1 strip along the long edges. Press. Piece a total of two strip sets measuring 2¾" × 42",

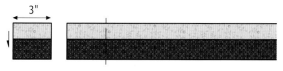

including the seam allowances. Crosscut the strip sets into 16 churn dash side segments, 3" wide.

Make 2 strip sets, 2¾" × 42".
Cut 16 segments, 3" wide.

2 Using the black #1 and cream 3⅛" triangles, follow step 2 of "Piecing the Quilt Center" on page 70 to piece 16 half-square-triangle units measuring 2¾" square, including the seam allowances.

3 Lay out four churn-dash side segments from step 1, four half-square-triangle units, and one assorted print 3" square in three horizontal rows. Join the pieces in each row. Press. Join the rows. Press. Repeat to piece a total of four Churn Dash blocks measuring 7½" square, including the seam allowances.

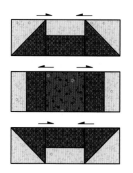 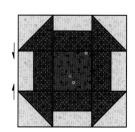

Make 4 Churn Dash blocks,
7½" × 7½".

4 Choosing the prints randomly, lay out 24 assorted print 2½" × 7½" rectangles side by side. Join the rectangles. Press. Repeat to piece a total of four piano-key rows measuring 7½" × 48½", including the seam allowances.

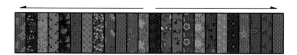

Make 4 piano-key rows, 7½" × 48½".

5 Referring to the borders diagram below, join a piano-key row to the right and left sides of the quilt center. Press.

6 Join a Churn Dash block to each end of the remaining two piano-key rows; press. Join these border rows to the top and bottom of the quilt center. Press.

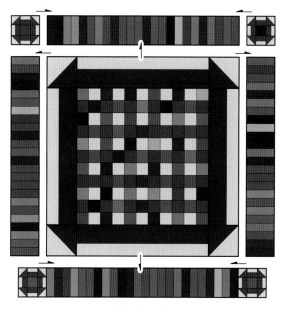

Adding borders

Completing the Quilt

Layer and baste the quilt top, batting, and backing. Quilt the layers. The featured quilt was machine quilted with a double apple-peel design in the pieced buffalo-plaid center of the quilt. The black churn-dash side strips were stitched with repeating straight lines, meeting in the black corner triangles where they formed Vs to fill the units. The cream background areas of the center churn dash were filled with a meandering feathered vine, and the piano-key border was stitched with a diagonal crosshatch. Referring to "Chubby Binding" on page 111, or substituting your own favorite method, use the black binding strips to bind the quilt.

Out of the Box

Plain meets pretty with these humble Churn Dash blocks fashioned from pairs of richly hued complementary prints. One of the best things about these blocks is they're secretly your best patchwork friend— with triangle points that "float" instead of resting against a seamline, you'll nail each and every one!

- - - - - - - -

FINISHED QUILT SIZE
17½" × 17½"

FINISHED BLOCK SIZE
5" × 5"

Materials

Yardage is based on 42" of usable fabric width after prewashing and removing selvages.

- ✦ 1 fat quarter (18" × 21") of cream print for blocks
- ✦ 18 chubby sixteenths (9" × 10½") of assorted prints for blocks, border, and binding
- ✦ ⅔ yard of fabric for backing
- ✦ 24" × 24" square of batting

Cutting

Cut all pieces across the width of the fabric in the order given unless otherwise noted.

From the cream print, cut:
9 strips, 1¼" × 8"
36 squares, 1¾" × 1¾"

From *each of 9* of the assorted prints, cut:
1 strip, 1" × 8" (combined total of 9; Churn Dash
    side rectangles)
Reserve the remainder of these assorted prints.

From *each of the remaining 9* assorted prints, cut:
5 squares, 1½" × 1½" (Churn Dash corner triangles and
    center square)
Keep the pieces organized by print. Reserve the remainder
    of these assorted prints.

Continued on page 74

Continued from page 73

From the remainder of all 18 assorted prints, cut a *combined total* of:
4 rectangles, 1½" × 5½" (border)*
4 rectangles, 1½" × 4½" (border)*
8 rectangles, 1½" × 3" (border)*
4 rectangles, 1½" × 2½" (border)*
18 rectangles, 1¼" × 4" (block frames)
36 rectangles, 1¼" × 3" (block frames)
Enough 2½"-wide rectangles in random lengths to
    make an 80" strip of binding when joined end
    to end (for my chubby-binding method provided
    on page 111, reduce the rectangle widths to 2")

*If you'd like to plan the placement of your prints,
rather than leave the positioning to chance, refer to
the border illustration on page 77 when cutting these
rectangles.*

Piecing the Framed Churn Dash Blocks

*Sew all pieces with right sides together using a ¼" seam
allowance unless otherwise noted. Press the seam
allowances as indicated by the arrows or otherwise
instructed.*

1 Select one print 1" × 8" strip, one cream
1¼" × 8" strip, four cream 1¾" squares,
and one set of five 1½" squares cut from a single
complementary print.

2 Join the cream and print strips along the long
edges to piece a strip set measuring 1¾" × 8",
including the seam allowances. Crosscut the strip set
into four segments, 1½" wide.

1½"

Make 1 strip set, 1¾" × 8".
Cut 4 segments, 1½" × 1¾".

3 Use a pencil and an acrylic ruler to draw a
diagonal sewing line from corner to corner
on the wrong side of four of the assorted print
1½" squares; set the remaining assorted print square
aside. Layer a prepared 1½" square onto a cream
1¾" square. Stitch the pair along the drawn line.
Press the resulting inner triangle open, aligning the
corner with the corner of the cream square. Press.
Trim away the layers beneath the top triangle, leaving
a ¼" seam allowance. Repeat to piece a total of four
units measuring 1¾" square, including the seam
allowances.

Make 4 units,
1¾" × 1¾".

4 Lay out the four pieced units, the four
strip-set segments from step 2, and the
reserved matching print 1½" square in three
horizontal rows. Join the pieces in each row. Press.
Join the rows. Press. The pieced churn-dash unit
should measure 4" square, including the seam
allowances.

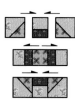

Churn-dash unit,
4" × 4"

5 Repeat steps 1–4 to piece a total of nine
churn-dash units.

6 Choosing the prints randomly, join a
1¼" × 4" rectangle to the right and left sides
of a churn-dash unit. Press the seam allowances
away from the churn dash. Randomly select four
print 1¼" × 3" rectangles. Join two rectangles along
the short ends. Press the seam allowances open.
Repeat to piece a total of two rectangles measuring
1¼" × 5½", including the seam allowances. Join these

 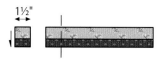

Finished quilt size: 17½" × 17½"
Finished block size: 5" × 5"

DESIGNED AND PIECED BY *Kim Diehl*
MACHINE QUILTED BY *Rebecca Silbaugh*

Stacked Patchwork: *To keep myself organized and enable me to easily stitch several blocks at once, I take a stacked approach to my patchwork. To do this, I repurpose a small portable cutting mat (or sometimes a large acrylic ruler—whatever is handy and will accommodate the size of my patchwork!) and lay out the components for each unit or block, stacking them one on top of the other up to six layers deep. Next, I begin working my way across each horizontal row, methodically pinning, stitching, and pressing the pieces, and using the mat to efficiently move everything between my different work areas. As I stitch the first components in a row, those that remain at the end of the row help me stay on track and serve as a placement guide for returning the stitched portions to my layout until each row is complete. Last, I join the rows to complete the block. This layered approach is super simple, effective, and helps me make quick progress!*

rectangles to the remaining sides of the churn dash unit. Press. The pieced Framed Churn Dash block should measure 5½" square, including the seam allowances.

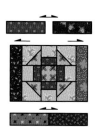

Framed Churn Dash block,
5½" × 5½"

7 Repeat step 6 to piece a total of nine Framed Churn Dash blocks.

Piecing the Quilt Center

Referring to the quilt-center assembly diagram below, lay out the blocks in three horizontal rows of three blocks, rotating every other block a quarter turn to achieve the featured design. Join the blocks in each row. Press. Join the rows. Press. The pieced quilt center should measure 15½" square, including the seam allowances.

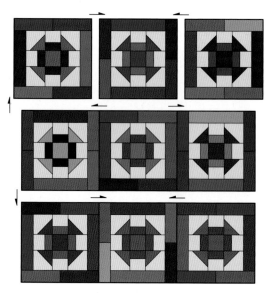

Quilt-center assembly

Piecing and Adding the Border

1 Lay out and join the assorted print rectangles in one horizontal row as shown. Press. Repeat to piece a total of two side borders measuring 1½" × 15½", including the seam allowances.

1½" × 3" 1½" × 4½" 1½" × 2½" 1½" × 4½" 1½" × 3"

Make 2 side borders, 1½" × 15½".

2 Lay out and join the remaining assorted print rectangles in one horizontal row as shown. Press. Repeat to piece a total of two top/bottom borders measuring 1½" × 17½", including the seam allowances.

1½" × 3" 1½" × 5½" 1½" × 2½" 1½" × 5½" 1½" × 3"

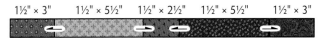

Make 2 top/bottom borders, 1½" × 17½".

3 Join the side borders to the right and left sides of the quilt center. Press. Join the top/bottom borders to the remaining sides of the quilt top. Press.

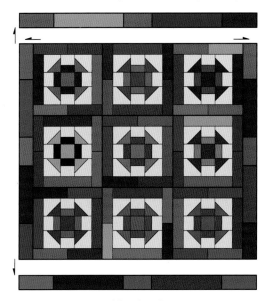

Adding borders

Completing the Quilt

Layer and baste the quilt top, batting, and backing. Quilt the layers. The featured quilt was machine quilted with an X in the center of each Framed Churn Dash block and V shapes radiating out from the side rectangles. Diagonal lines were stitched through the dark and light triangles at each corner of the blocks. An egg-and-dart design was stitched over the block frames and borders. Referring to "Chubby Binding" on page 111, or substituting your own favorite method, join the assorted print 2½"-wide random-length rectangles to make a pieced strip, and use it to bind the quilt.

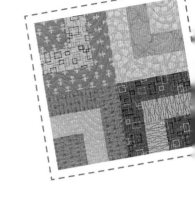

Four Square

Geometry lends a bit of a mosaic vibe in this king-size quilt brimming with strippy, scrappy, modern-day charm. Plumped-up patchwork and oversized blocks are lickety-split fast to stitch and beautifully showcase a dazzling array of prints.

— — — — — — — —

FINISHED QUILT SIZE
108½" × 108½"

FINISHED BLOCK SIZE
18" × 18"

Materials

Yardage is based on 42" of usable fabric width after prewashing and removing selvages.

- ✦ 2 yards of dark print for blocks and binding
- ✦ ¾ yard *each* of 21 assorted prints for blocks
- ✦ 9¾ yards of fabric for backing
- ✦ 117" × 117" square of batting

pin point

Pared Down Prints: *For my quilt, I chose to include a dark print for the binding and use it to cut three sets of block patchwork pieces as noted in "Cutting" on page 80 for more drama. For fewer leftover scraps from the 21 assorted prints, the dark binding print can be reduced to ¾ yard, in keeping with the other prints, bringing the total number of assorted prints to 22. Referring again to "Cutting," one complete set of block patchwork pieces can be cut from each of the 22 assorted prints used, with one additional set of patchwork pieces cut from each of your 14 favorites. For a deliciously scrappy binding option, cut enough 2½"-wide strips in random lengths from scraps of all 22 assorted prints to make a 440" length of binding and … you're all set!*

Cutting

Cut all pieces across the width of the fabric in the order given unless otherwise noted.

From the dark print, cut:

2 strips, 4½" × 42"; crosscut into 12 squares,
   4½" × 4½"

9 strips, 3" × 42"; crosscut into:
- 12 rectangles, 3" × 9½"
- 24 rectangles, 3" × 7"
- 12 rectangles, 3" × 4½"

11 binding strips, 2½" × 42" (for my chubby-binding method provided on page 111, reduce the strip width to 2")

Note: The 3" and 4½" pieces cut from the dark print make up three complete sets of block patchwork; please keep them grouped together for the piecing steps.

From *each* of the 21 assorted prints, cut 1 set of:

1 strip, 4½" × 42"; crosscut into 4 squares, 4½" × 4½"
   (combined total of 84)

3 strips, 3" × 42"; crosscut into:
- 4 rectangles, 3" × 9½" (combined total of 84)
- 8 rectangles, 3" × 7" (combined total of 168)
- 4 rectangles, 3" × 4½" (combined total of 84)

From *each* of 12 assorted prints, cut:

3 strips, 3" × 42"; crosscut into:
- 4 rectangles, 3" × 9½" (combined total of 132, including the previously cut rectangles)
- 8 rectangles, 3" × 7" (combined total of 264, including the previously cut rectangles)
- 4 rectangles, 3" × 4½" (combined total of 132, including the previously cut rectangles)

4 squares, 4½" × 4½" (combined total of 132, including the previously cut squares; these squares can be cut from the remainder of each original 4½" × 42" strip)

Keep the patchwork sets organized by print.

pin point

Choosing a Perfect Blend of Prints:
The perfect blend of prints for any given project is surely subjective, and in my mind there are absolutely no right or wrong choices—use what makes you happy! I firmly believe in trusting my instincts and pleasing myself when it comes to gathering my prints, but I do use a few simple guidelines to help me make successful choices.

It may sound overly simple, but when I look at the prints and colors I've gathered and instantly love the mix, I run with it … no second-guessing myself! However, if I'm less than sure about what I've pulled together, and I'm on the fence about whether it's a good blend, this is a loud and clear sign that I need to make changes.

After choosing my basic color scheme, I begin considering how to build a nice variety of textures and scale for the prints to work together successfully as a group. Choosing fabrics that are all of a similar scale, whether large or small, would produce a very "one note" look and the pieced blocks would appear muddled and lack definition. For a good degree of contrast and interest, the "formula" I use is to primarily choose medium-scale prints in a variety of textures (geometrics, florals, stripes, dots), and include a handful each of smaller-scale and larger-scale prints to add a little sizzle and pop. These guidelines work really well for me, and I'm sharing them in the hopes that they'll work really well for you too!

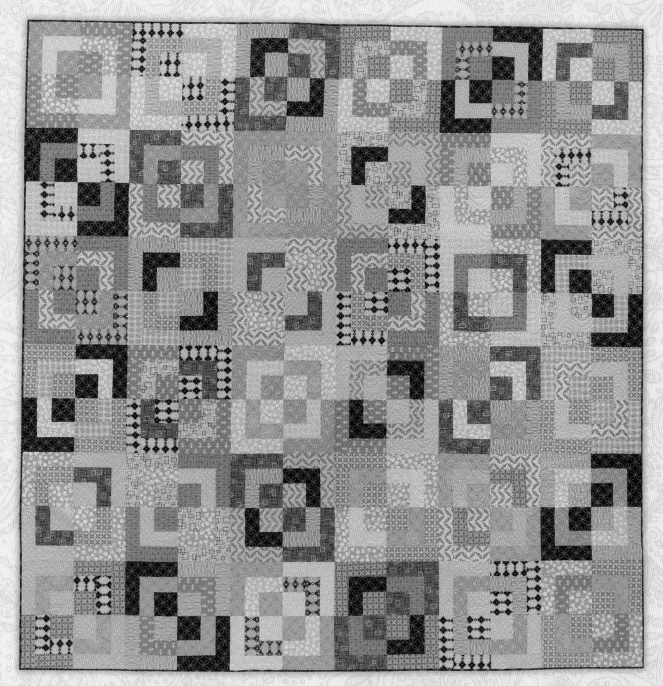

Finished quilt size: 108½" × 108½"
Finished block size: 18" × 18"

DESIGNED AND PIECED BY *Kim Diehl*
MACHINE QUILTED BY *Connie Tabor*

Piecing the Four Square Blocks

*Sew all pieces with right sides together using a ¼"
seam allowance unless otherwise noted. Press the seam
allowances as indicated by the arrows.*

1 From the group of 22 assorted prints,
including the dark binding print, select four
complete sets of patchwork pieces cut from four
different prints. From one print, choose two 4½"
squares, two 3" × 7" rectangles, and two 3" × 9½"
rectangles. From a second print, choose two 3" × 4½"
rectangles and two 3" × 7" rectangles. Stack the pieces
one on top of another as shown; when stitched, these
pieces will form two matching block quarter units.
Repeat with the remaining two chosen prints to form
four layers of patchwork. Return the remainder of all
four sets of prints to the original group of 22.

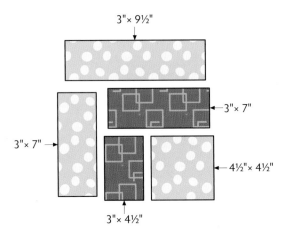

3"× 9½"

3"× 7"

3"× 7"

4½"× 4½"

3"× 4½"

2 Join and press the patchwork pieces as shown,
working through each layer, to piece a total
of four block quarter units measuring 9½" square,
including the seam allowances.

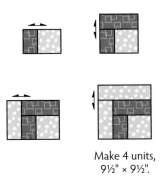

Make 4 units,
9½" × 9½".

3 Lay out the four block quarter units in two horizontal rows as shown. Join the units in each row. Press. Join the rows. Press. The pieced Four Square block should measure 18½" square, including the seam allowances.

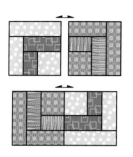 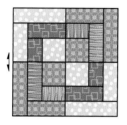

Four Square block,
18½" × 18½"

4 Repeat steps 1–3, selecting a different combination of four prints for each block to piece a total of 36 blocks.

Piecing the Quilt Top

Lay out the blocks in six horizontal rows of six blocks each. Join the blocks in each row. Press. Join the rows. Press.

Completing the Quilt

Layer and baste the quilt top, batting, and backing. Quilt the layers. The featured quilt was machine quilted with a large-scale edge-to-edge design of repeating gentle S curves, with small strings of pearls stitched into the center row of each cluster of curves. Referring to "Chubby Binding" on page 111, or substituting your own favorite method, use the dark binding strips (or the pieced scrappy binding, if you've chosen to use the option provided in the Pin Point tip on page 79) to bind the quilt.

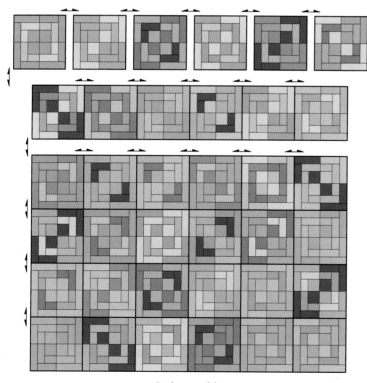

Quilt assembly

Gosh and Golly

Gather the smallest saved scraps from your favorite prints, stitch them into an assortment of patchwork bits and blocks, and then fashion them into this sweet little sampler quilt. Simple stitching, a variety of techniques, and a range of patchwork styles will keep you entertained from start to finish!

- - - - - - -

FINISHED QUILT SIZE:
21½" × 24½"

Materials

Yardage is based on 42" of usable fabric width after prewashing and removing selvages.

- ✦ Approximately ⅞ yard *total* of assorted dark print scraps for patchwork
- ✦ Appoximately ½ yard *total* of assorted light print scraps for patchwork
- ✦ ⅜ yard of black print for inner border, outer border corner squares, and binding
- ✦ ¼ yard (not a fat quarter) of cranberry stripe or print for outer border
- ✦ ¾ yard of fabric for backing
- ✦ 27" × 30" rectangle of batting

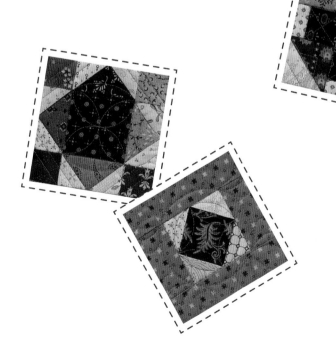

Cutting for Blocks and Units

All patchwork pieces are cut from the assorted prints. Refer to the quilt photo on page 89 when cutting your prints, or create your own color scheme. To simplify these steps, I chose to cut fabrics and piece the blocks one style at a time. If you prefer to cut everything at once, keep the pieces organized as you cut them.

Framed Square-in-a-Square Blocks

2 dark squares, 2½" × 2½"

8 light squares, 1½" × 1½"

2 sets, each cut from a single dark print:
- ✦ 2 rectangles, 1½" × 2½" (combined total of 4)
- ✦ 2 rectangles, 1½" × 4½" (combined total of 4)

Framed Hourglass Blocks and Unit

6 light squares, 3¼" × 3¼"; cut each square in half diagonally *twice* to yield 4 triangles (total of 24)

6 dark squares, 3¼" × 3¼"; cut each square in half diagonally *twice* to yield 4 triangles (total of 24)

4 dark rectangles, 1½" × 2½"

4 dark rectangles, 1½" × 4½"

Large Flying-Geese Units

2 light rectangles, 2½" × 4½"

4 dark squares, 2½" × 2½"

Small Flying-Geese Units

11 light rectangles, 1½" × 2½"

22 dark squares, 1½" × 1½"

Small Star Block

1 dark square, 2½" × 2½"

4 light rectangles, 1½" × 2½"

8 dark squares, 1½" × 1½"

4 light squares, 1½" × 1½"

Large Star Block

1 dark square, 3½" × 3½"

4 light rectangles, 2" × 3½"

8 dark squares, 2" × 2"

4 light squares, 2" × 2"

Large Pinwheel Block

4 light squares, 2⅞" × 2⅞"; cut each square in half diagonally *once* to yield 2 triangles (total of 8)

4 dark squares, 2⅞" × 2⅞"; cut each square in half diagonally *once* to yield 2 triangles (total of 8)

Framed Small Pinwheel Block

4 light squares, 2½" × 2½"; cut each square in half diagonally *once* to yield 2 triangles (total of 8)

4 dark squares, 2½" × 2½"; cut each square in half diagonally *once* to yield 2 triangles (total of 8)

4 dark rectangles, 1½" × 2½"

4 light squares, 1½" × 1½"

4 dark rectangles, 1½" × 4½"

Churn Dash Block

4 light squares, 2⅞" × 2⅞"; cut each square in half diagonally *once* to yield 2 triangles (total of 8)

4 dark squares, 2⅞" × 2⅞"; cut each square in half diagonally *once* to yield 2 triangles (total of 8)

1 light strip, 1" × 8"

1 dark strip, 1½" × 8"

1 light square, 1½" × 1½"

King's Crown Block

1 dark square, 2½" × 2½"

4 dark rectangles, 1½" × 2½"

8 light squares, 1½" × 1½"

4 dark squares, 1½" × 1½"

Rail Fence Block

3 dark rectangles, 1½" × 3½"

Rail Fence Variation Block

3 assorted squares, 1½" × 1½"

2 dark rectangles, 1½" × 3½"

Pieced Rectangle Unit

2 rectangles, 1½" × 4½"

Checkerboard Squares

36 assorted squares, 1½" × 1½"

Cutting for Borders and Binding

From the black print, cut:

2 strips, 1" × 42"; crosscut into:

+ 2 strips, 1" × 19½"
+ 2 strips, 1" × 17½"

3 strips, 2½" × 42"; from *1 of the strips*, cut 4 squares, 2½" × 2½". Reserve the remainder of this strip and the other black 2½" × 42" strips for the binding (for my chubby-binding method provided on page 111, reduce the strip width to 2").

From the cranberry stripe or print, cut:

2 strips, 2½" × 42"; crosscut into:

+ 2 strips, 2½" × 20½"
+ 2 strips, 2½" × 17½"

Piecing the Blocks and Units

Sew all pieces with right sides together using a ¼" seam allowance unless otherwise noted. Press the seam allowances as indicated by the arrows or otherwise specified.

FRAMED SQUARE-IN-A-SQUARE BLOCKS

1 Use a pencil and an acrylic ruler to draw a diagonal sewing line from corner to corner on the wrong side of each light 1½" square.

2 To sew the stitch-and-fold triangle corners, layer a prepared square onto opposite corners of a dark 2½" center square. Stitch the squares along the drawn lines. Fold the resulting inner triangles open, aligning the corners with the corners of the bottom square. Press. Trim away the excess layers underneath the top triangles, leaving ¼" seam allowances. In the same manner, add a light triangle

to the two remaining dark corners. The pieced square-in-a-square unit should measure 2½" square, including the seam allowances.

Square-in-a-square unit,
2½" × 2½"

3 Join the dark 1½" × 2½" rectangles and 1½" × 4½" rectangles to the square-in-a-square unit as shown. Press. The pieced block should measure 4½" square, including the seam allowances. Repeat to piece a total of two blocks.

Make 2 Framed Square-in-a-Square blocks,
4½" × 4½".

FRAMED HOURGLASS BLOCKS

1 Select two light and two dark 3¼" triangles cut for one hourglass unit. Join the triangles as shown. Press and trim away the dog-ear points. Repeat to piece a total of three hourglass units measuring 2½" square, including the seam allowances. The remaining triangles will be unused.

Make 3 units,
2½" × 2½".

2 Join a dark 1½" × 2½" rectangle to the right and left sides of an hourglass unit. Press. Join a dark 1½" × 4½" rectangle to each remaining side of the hourglass unit. Press. Repeat to piece a total of two Framed Hourglass blocks measuring 4½" square, including the seam allowances. Reserve the remaining hourglass unit for later use.

Make 2 Framed Hourglass blocks,
4½" × 4½".

LARGE AND SMALL FLYING-GEESE UNITS

1 Select one light 2½" × 4½" rectangle and two dark 2½" squares. Draw a diagonal sewing line from corner to corner on the wrong side of each 2½" square as previously instructed. Following the stitch-and-fold-triangle technique outlined in step 2 of "Framed Square-in-a-Square Blocks" on page 87, use the prepared squares and 2½" × 4½" rectangle to sew a large flying-geese unit measuring 2½" × 4½", including the seam allowances. Repeat to piece a total of two large flying-geese units.

Make 2 units,
2½" × 4½".

2 Using one light 1½" × 2½" rectangle and two dark 1½" squares, repeat step 1 to piece 11 small flying-geese units measuring 1½" × 2½", including the seam allowances.

Make 11 units,
1½" × 2½".

88

Finished quilt size: 21½" × 24½"

DESIGNED AND PIECED BY *Kim Diehl*
MACHINE QUILTED BY *Rebecca Silbaugh*

SMALL AND LARGE STAR BLOCKS

1 Using the pieces cut for the Small Star block, draw a diagonal sewing line from corner to corner on the wrong side of each dark 1½" square as previously instructed. Following the stitch-and-fold-triangle technique outlined in step 2 of "Framed Square-in-a-Square Blocks," use the prepared dark squares and four light 1½" × 2½" rectangles to piece four flying-geese star-point units measuring 1½" × 2½", including the seam allowances.

Make 4 units,
1½" × 2½".

2 Lay out the flying-geese star-point units, four light 1½" squares, and one dark 2½" square in three horizontal rows as shown. Join the pieces in each row. Press. Join the rows. Press. The Small Star block should measure 4½" square, including the seam allowances.

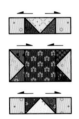

Small Star block,
4½" × 4½"

3 Using the pieces cut for the Large Star block, repeat steps 1 and 2 to stitch one Large Star block measuring 6½" square, including seam allowances.

LARGE PINWHEEL BLOCK AND FRAMED SMALL PINWHEEL BLOCK

1 Select four light and four dark triangles cut for the Large Pinwheel block. Join a light triangle to a dark triangle along the long diagonal edges. Press. Trim away the dog-ear points. Repeat

to piece a total of four half-square-triangle units measuring 2½" square, including the seam allowances.

Make 4 units,
2½" × 2½".

2 Lay out the half-square-triangle units in two horizontal rows of two squares. Join the squares in each row. Press. Join the rows. Press. The Large Pinwheel block should measure 4½" square, including the seam allowances.

Large Pinwheel block,
4½" × 4½"

3 Using four light and four dark triangles cut for the Framed Small Pinwheel block, repeat step 2 to make a second pinwheel unit. Use a rotary cutter and acrylic ruler to trim down the unit size to 2½" square, including the seam allowances. The remaining triangles will be unused.

Trim pinwheel unit to
2½" × 2½".

4 Select the remaining pieces cut for the Framed Small Pinwheel block. Lay out the trimmed pinwheel unit, four dark 1½" × 2½" rectangles, and four light 1½" squares in three horizontal rows. Join the pieces in each row. Press. Join the rows. Press. Sew two dark 1½" × 4½"

rectangles to the right and left sides of the patchwork unit, and two dark 1½" × 6½" rectangles to the remaining sides of the unit, pressing after each pair of rectangles is added. The pieced Framed Small Pinwheel block should measure 6½" square, including the seam allowances.

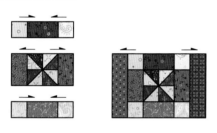

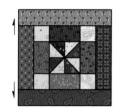

Framed Small Pinwheel block,
6½" × 6½"

CHURN DASH BLOCK

1 Using the pieces cut for the Churn Dash blocks, join a light triangle and a dark triangle along the long diagonal edges. Press. Trim away the dog-ear points. Repeat to piece a total of four half-square-triangle units measuring 2" square, including the seam allowances. The remaining triangles will be unused.

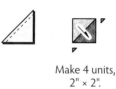

Make 4 units,
2" × 2".

2 Join the light 1" × 8" and the black 1½" × 8" strips along the long edges. Press. Crosscut the strip set into four segments, 1½" wide.

Cut 4 segments.

3 Lay out the step 1 and 2 units with the light 1½" square in three horizontal rows. Join the pieces in each row. Press. Join the rows. Press. The Churn Dash block should measure 4½" square, including the seam allowances.

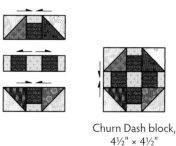

Churn Dash block,
4½" × 4½"

KING'S CROWN BLOCK

Using the pieces cut for the King's Crown block, draw a diagonal sewing line on the wrong side of the eight light 1½" squares as previously instructed. Following the stitch-and-fold-triangle technique outlined in step 2 of "Framed Square-in-a-Square Blocks" on page 87, use the prepared squares and dark 1½" × 2½" rectangles to sew four flying-geese units measuring 1½" × 2½", including the seam allowances. Lay out the flying-geese units, four dark 1½" squares, and one dark 2½" square in three horizontal rows. Join the pieces in each row. Press. Join the rows. Press. The King's Crown block should measure 4½" square, including the seam allowances.

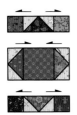

King's Crown block,
4½" × 4½"

RAIL FENCE AND
RAIL FENCE VARIATION BLOCKS

Using the pieces cut for the Rail Fence block, join the rectangles. Press. Repeat using the pieces for the Rail Fence Variation block, joining the pieces in three horizontal rows. The pieced Rail Fence and Rail Fence Variation blocks should measure 3½" square, including the seam allowances.

Rail Fence block and variation

PIECED RECTANGLE UNIT

Join the two rectangles cut for the pieced rectangle unit along the long edges. Press. The unit should measure 2½" × 4½", including the seam allowances.

Pieced rectangle unit

Assembling the Quilt Center

1 Select 12 assorted 1½" squares cut for the checkerboard. Join and press four squares to make a four-patch unit, and the remaining eight squares to make a checkerboard unit.

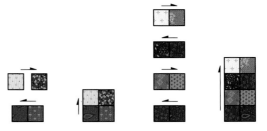

Make 1 four-patch unit,
2½" × 2½".

Make 1 checkerboard unit,
2½" × 4½".

2 Lay out the section 1 components as shown; join and press. Section 1 should measure 6½" × 8½", including the seam allowances.

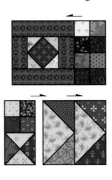 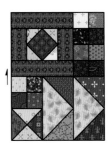

Section 1,
6½" × 8½"

Simple Patchwork

3 Lay out the section 2 components as shown; join and press. Section 2 should measure 4½" × 8½", including the seam allowances.

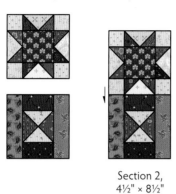

Section 2,
4½" × 8½"

4 Choosing the prints randomly, select six assorted 1½" squares cut for the checkerboard; join and press to make a checkerboard unit measuring 2½" × 3½", including the seam allowances.

Make 1 unit,
2½" × 3½".

5 Lay out the checkerboard unit and the remaining section 3 components as shown; join and press. Section 3 should measure 6½" × 8½", including the seam allowances.

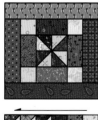
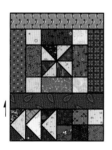

Section 3,
6½" × 8½"

6 Select a random mix of four assorted 1½" squares cut for the checkerboard; join and press to make a checkerboard unit measuring

1½" × 4½", including the seam allowances. Lay out the checkerboard unit with the remaining section 4 components as shown; join and press. Section 4 should measure 6½" × 11½", including the seam allowances.

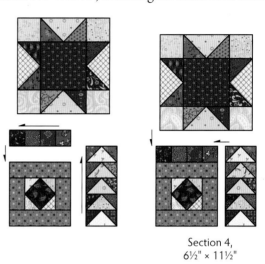

Section 4,
6½" × 11½"

7 Choosing the prints randomly, select 12 assorted 1½" squares cut for the checkerboard; join and press to make a checkerboard unit measuring 3½" × 4½", including the seam allowances. Lay out the checkerboard unit with the remaining section 5 components as shown; join and press. Section 5 should measure 4½" × 11½", including the seam allowances.

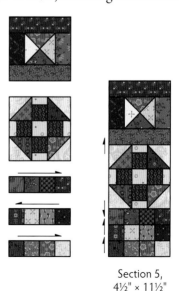

Section 5,
4½" × 11½"

Adding the Borders

1 Join a black 1" × 19½" strip to the right and left sides of the quilt center. Press. Join a black 1" × 17½" strip to the top and bottom edges of the quilt center. Press.

2 Sew a cranberry 2½" × 20½" strip to the right and left sides of the quilt top. Press. Join a black 2½" square to each end of the cranberry 2½" × 17½" strips. Press. Join these strips to the top and bottom edges of the quilt top. Press.

8 Select the remaining two assorted print 1½" squares cut for the checkerboard; join and press to make a two-patch unit measuring 1½" × 2½", including the seam allowances. Lay out the section 6 components as shown; join and press. Section 6 should measure 6½" × 11½", including the seam allowances.

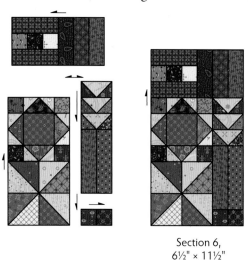

Section 6,
6½" × 11½"

Quilt assembly

9 Referring to the pictured quilt on page 89 and the quilt assembly diagram below, lay out sections 1, 2, and 3 to form the top half of the quilt center. Join the sections. Press the seam allowances open. In the same manner, join and press sections 4, 5, and 6 to form the bottom half of the quilt center. Join the top and bottom halves to complete the quilt center. Press the seam allowances open. The pieced quilt center should measure 16½" × 19½", including the seam allowances.

Completing the Quilt

Layer and baste the quilt top, batting, and backing. Quilt the layers. The featured quilt was machine quilted with a variety of traditional and whimsical designs to suit each section of patchwork. The striped print inspired the quilting design for the outer border, with the curvy stripes outlined for texture. Referring to "Chubby Binding" on page 111, or substituting your own favorite method, use the black binding strips to bind the quilt.

Cabin Garland

TABLE RUNNER

Raid your scrap basket, gather together those last saved bits of your favorite prints, and stitch them into this table runner of log cabin–inspired strips and patchwork diamonds. This small and simply pieced quilt comes together so quickly, it can be started *and* finished in a single day—my kind of project!

- - - - - - - -

FINISHED QUILT SIZE
12½" × 28½"

FINISHED BLOCK SIZE
4" × 12"

Materials

Yardage is based on 42" of usable fabric width after prewashing and removing selvages.

- ✦ Approximately ½ yard of assorted print scraps for patchwork
- ✦ ½ yard of black print for patchwork and binding
- ✦ ½ yard of fabric for backing
- ✦ 18" × 35" rectangle of batting

Cutting

Cut all pieces across the width of the fabric in the order given unless otherwise noted.

From the assorted print scraps, cut:
56 rectangles, 1½" × 6"

From the black print, cut:
5 strips, 2½" × 42"; crosscut 2 strips into 14 rectangles, 2½" × 5½". Reserve the remaining strips for the binding (for my chubby-binding technique provided on page 111, reduce the width of the binding strips to 2").

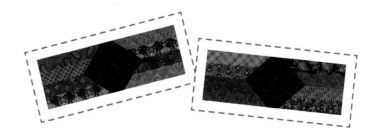

DESIGNED AND PIECED BY *Kim Diehl*
MACHINE QUILTED BY *Lois Walker*

pin point

Toeing the Line: For patchwork units with drawn lines, I snap on the open-toe presser foot. The open center area of the foot creates a nice little "window," enabling me to clearly see and easily follow the drawn lines for accurate results. If you don't have an open-toe foot, a presser foot with a clear acrylic center is the next best thing!

Piecing the Patchwork Units

Sew all pieces with right sides together using a ¼" seam allowance unless otherwise noted. Press the seam allowances as indicated by the arrows or otherwise instructed.

1 Choosing the prints randomly, join two rectangles along the long edges. Press. Repeat to piece a total of 28 rectangle units measuring 2½" × 6", including the seam allowances.

Make 28 units,
2½" × 6".

2 Position a black 2½" × 5½" rectangle onto a pieced rectangle unit as shown. Use a pencil and an acrylic ruler to draw a diagonal sewing line from the corner of the black rectangle to the opposite edge where the pieced rectangle corner rests underneath; pin the pair together. Stitch the pair exactly *next* to the drawn line, on the side closest to the black corner. Fold the black rectangle open, aligning the side edges with the pieced rectangle underneath to keep it square. Press. Once the fabric

has cooled, flip the black rectangle back to expose the sewn seam, and trim away the excess corner layers leaving a ¼" seam allowance. Repeat to piece a total of seven partial A units measuring 2½" × 9", including the seam allowances.

Make 7 partial A units,
2½" × 9".

3 Repeat step 2, positioning the pieces as shown, to piece seven partial B units measuring 2½" × 9", including the seam allowances.

Make 7 partial B units,
2½" × 9".

4 Use a partial A unit from step 2 and a pieced rectangle unit from step 1 to complete the unit as shown. Repeat to piece a total of seven A units measuring 2½" × 12½", including seam allowances.

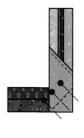  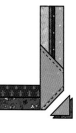

Make 7 A units,
2½" × 12½".

Cabin Garland Table Runner **97**

5 Select a partial B unit from step 3 and a pieced rectangle unit from step 1. Using the illustration as a guide, complete the units as previously instructed. Repeat to piece a total of seven B units measuring 2½" × 12½", including the seam allowances.

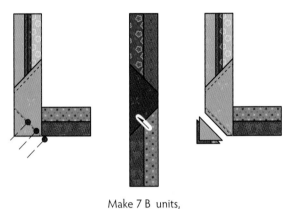

Make 7 B units,
2½" × 12½".

Piecing the Table Runner

1 Select an A unit and a B unit. With the units layered right sides together, align and pin the black seams at the wide side of the black half-diamond shapes. Continue working out from each pinned black seam to the ends of the unit to complete the pinning. Stitch the pair along the pinned edge. Press. Repeat to piece a total of seven Diamond blocks measuring 4½" × 12½", including the seam allowances.

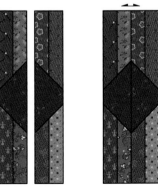

Make 7 Diamond blocks,
4½" × 12½".

2 Lay out the seven Diamond blocks side by side. Join the blocks. Press.

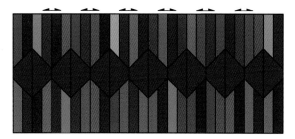

Table-runner assembly

pin point

Coordinating Place Mats: This Cabin Garland Table Runner pattern can easily be adapted to stitch place mats for a complete table set. For each mat, cut 32 rectangles, 1½" × 6", from approximately ⅓ yard of assorted print scraps, and 8 rectangles, 2½" × 5½", from ¼ yard of black print. Follow the table runner instructions to stitch and join four Diamond blocks to make a place mat measuring 12½" × 16½". Layer, baste, and quilt the mat as desired, and use the remainder of the black print to bind it. Repeat as needed!

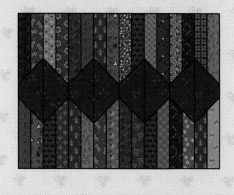

Completing the Table Runner

Layer and baste the table-runner top, batting, and backing. Quilt the layers. The featured quilt was machine quilted with a repeating pattern of straight lines echoing out from the seams of the black diamonds to form a zigzag design. The black diamond centers were stitched with a basket weave pattern to produce a checkerboard texture.

For added interest, I trimmed away each corner of the table runner at a 45° angle. If you choose to trim away the corners of your table runner as well, measure down 2" from the corner at each short end and use a pencil to mark this position. Use a rotary cutter and acrylic ruler to make a cut from the outer edge of the second rectangle seam from each corner of the table runner, extending diagonally to the mark. Referring to "Chubby Binding" on page 111, or substituting your own favorite method, use the black binding strips to bind the quilt.

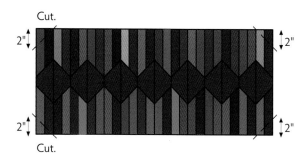

Cut.
2"   2"
2"   2"
Cut.

Kim's Favorite Tips, Tricks, Hints, and Helps

I've been blessed to have quiltmaking in my life for more than 20 years now, and I can honestly say I love it just as much today as I did when I stitched my very first block. Truth be told, I might even love quiltmaking more *now*, because my years of experience have helped me amass a nice little bundle of quiltmaking tricks for accurate stitching. Many of these are simple things, combining my commonsense approach to quiltmaking with small steps that produce big results.

In the pages that follow, I've gathered and shared my favorite tips, tricks, hints, and helps. I hope that you'll find them useful as well, and that they'll make your stitching time efficient, productive, and enjoyable!

~ *Kim*

Fabric Organization

If I'm shopping to plump up my stash, rather than purchasing the prints needed for a specific project, I've learned to focus on fat quarters and buy in balance. This means that as I'm choosing my fat quarters, I'll grab a red print, then a blue print, then a green print, and so on, continuing until I've accumulated a nice sampling of prints in a huge variety of colors. Buying in balance means that my on-hand stash will also be in balance, and I can easily pull prints to accommodate any project.

A convenient way to organize my precuts is to use an over-the-door shoe organizer with clear acrylic pockets. I like grouping the prints by color and rolling them to fit the pockets, which enables tons of prints to be tucked into each one. Best of all, this approach lets me see at a glance what I have on hand.

When I *really* love a particular print, I'll typically buy it in 1- or 2-yard increments—or sometimes more! Because wrangling large cuts of fabric around the cutting table can be awkward, for my first use I generally cut a ½-yard piece and then subcut this into two fat quarters. Later, if I need a fat eighth or a chubby sixteenth (my term for half of a fat eighth), I can subcut these pieces from one

fat quarter, and return the leftover pieces that are now in standard precut sizes back to my stash. This approach helps build a good variety of prints in often-called-for sizes, making it a snap to pull prints for any given scrap project.

Preparing Fabrics for Cutting

To speed the cutting process, I like to use layered stacks of prints. To build a stack, I place my first print (one without a pronounced grid or stripe) on the pressing surface and give it a quick press with a hot, dry iron. I then continue adding and pressing the prints one layer at a time, up to six layers deep, to sandwich them firmly together for cutting. As the stack is built, I make sure the prints are aligned along one raw edge and the selvages are resting one on top of the other to ensure the grain of the fabric runs consistently in the same direction. If my mix of prints includes one with a strong gridded pattern or stripe, I place it as my top layer so that I can position it well for cutting and eliminate crooked lines. Last, I transfer the pressed stack of prints to my cutting mat, aligning the pattern of the top print or stripe with the grid of the mat to ensure it's resting in a straight position, and begin making the cuts.

For small-scale patchwork projects, I prepare my stacks of prints for cutting as previously described, but with the addition of one small step. As I add each new layer, I give it a light mist of Best Press (a starch alternative) before smoothing it with the iron. Best Press adds body and firms up the texture of the fabric, stabilizing it beautifully for the piecing steps.

Patchwork Tips

I've learned through the years that using a ¼" presser foot doesn't necessarily guarantee an accurately stitched ¼" seam allowance. After comparing several ¼" presser feet side by side, I was surprised to discover that the guide on each one can be slightly different. In addition, how gently or firmly the fabric rests against the presser foot guide for stitching can also affect the results. To help me achieve accuracy, from time to time I stitch a quick test piece using three rectangles, 1½" × 3", and join them along the long edges. After pressing the seam allowances away from the center rectangle, it should measure 1" wide. If it measures differently, I adjust the placement of my subsequent patchwork pieces when feeding them through the sewing machine, as dictated by my results.

For patchwork seams that are sturdy, secure, *and* invisible, I rely on a combination of two elements. First, I slightly reduce the stitch length on my sewing machine from the standard setting of 2.2 down to 1.8 (even for larger-scale patchwork!) because the smaller stitches are less visible and will remain secure at the patchwork edges. Next, I use a neutral thread color (*never* white), because once the seam allowances have been pressed, bits of thread along the sewn seam can occasionally become visible. White thread will stand out against your prints, whereas neutral tones will be much less noticeable. I use a khaki color for warmer, deeper-hued prints and gray for cooler, brighter prints.

When I layer and pin my units together for stitching, I *always* place a glass-head pin at the end of each unit, about ¼" from the bottom edge. As I'm completing the stitching and approaching the end of the unit, I lay my fingertip over the pin head and use it to guide the piece under the presser foot in a straight position, slowing the sewing machine to a crawl to avoid striking the pin. This little trick helps eliminate fishtailing and enables me to achieve a consistent seam-allowance width from edge to edge.

I routinely chain piece my patchwork units as described on page 108 to speed the stitching steps. For even more efficiency, I use thread snips, rather than traditional scissors, to quickly cut the pieced units apart with a small squeeze of my fingers. Snips are a great time-saver!

For stitched seams with a lot of bulk (often from units with multiple pieced layers or stitched triangle points), I've learned that pressing the seam allowances open is an option that should always be considered. Pressing the seams open minimizes and disperses the bulk.

When I'm laying out and auditioning the placement of my pieced blocks to form the quilt center, I've learned that blocks with muted or subtle colors can appear to fade away when placed in the corners, and the quilt center will sometimes lack definition. Positioning blocks with strong colors in the corners helps anchor the design and defines the quilt center beautifully. (Ditto for border units!)

Successful Scrap Quilts

For scrap quilt designs that specify the number of patchwork pieces to be cut, I'll often cut a handful of extra pieces in each given size (scraps permitting). Having a few extra pieces on hand gives me options as I pair up the pieces for my last needed units, and it also gives me the ability to toss out any piece with a print that looks crooked or is flawed in any way, without having to interrupt my stitching to cut more.

When I'm choosing prints randomly from a cut assortment of patchwork pieces and chain piecing them into scrappy units, I like to pause when I have a handful of units remaining (about a dozen, more or less) and determine what my final print pairings will be. A little preplanning near the end of each piecing step means that I'll always be pleased with the look of my stitched units, and this eliminates less-than-ideal print combinations.

Once I'm pleased with my block arrangement and I'm ready to piece the blocks into rows or larger units, I've discovered that I can ditch my old-fashioned method of writing and pinning notes onto units to keep them straight. Instead, I use my smart phone or digital camera for an easy visual reference. Snapping a quick picture of the layout provides a convenient guide for easy patchwork assembly, and it helps keep my units positioned exactly as I intended them. Another bonus to using a digital photo for layout purposes is that any misstep in the choice or positioning of prints will be glaringly apparent when viewed through the camera's eye. Seeing missteps *before* the units are joined enables me to easily make changes and eliminates "unsewing" them.

Incorporating "zinger" prints (meaning prints that aren't similar to the rest) can work a little bit of magic in your quilts, so don't be afraid to include these. I've learned, though, that the secret to using zingers successfully is to always use them more than once. One zinger can look like an accident and appear out of place, while using it twice or more at spaced intervals across the top will give the finished quilt a thoughtful, intentional, and balanced appearance.

Stitch-and-Fold Triangles

To eliminate drawing diagonal sewing lines from corner to corner on the wrong side of patchwork squares measuring typically less than 2½" to 3" (depending upon the size of your sewing-machine surface), I like to create a sewing guide using tape or permanent marker. To do this, lower the sewing-machine needle to the down position, rest the edge of an acrylic ruler against the left side of the needle (ensuring it's resting in a straight line), and lower the presser foot to hold it in place. Run a strip of 1"-wide painter's tape exactly along the ruler's edge, taking care not to cover the feed dogs, or use a fine-tipped permanent black marker to draw a sewing line exactly along the ruler's edge. As I sew each stitch-and-fold triangle unit, I align the front point of the layered square with the sewing-machine needle, and the opposite bottom corner of the square with the drawn line or tape edge. As I slide the unit along and stitch the layers, I keep the bottom point of the square positioned on the drawn line or tape edge, enabling me to sew exactly through the center of the square and eliminate the need for drawn sewing lines. This trick is a *huge* time-saver!

I reposition the unit and ruler and repeat with the remaining corner to trim the patchwork to the specified size. This approach produces precisely sized units and removes the dog-ear points at the same time. Adding this quick step *now* can save a tremendous amount of time later!

Despite our best efforts, occasionally the edges of a stitch-and-fold triangle won't quite reach the corner of the unit it's stitched to, so it doesn't align properly when folded open. If this occurs, rather than unsew and resew the unit, I've learned to trim away the middle layer of fabric *only*, leaving the bottom rectangle or square layer intact. The benefit of this approach is that your finished unit will retain its original accurate size, simplifying the remaining patchwork steps.

Half-Square-Triangle Units

When I layer my triangles for stitching, if there's a discrepancy in the sizes, I always align the pieces at the squared corner rather than at the long diagonal edges. Layering the pieces in this way ensures that any size differences will be absorbed into the seam allowances when the unit is stitched together.

I've met many quiltmakers who like to cut their triangles larger than needed and then trim them to size after stitching. I've never been a fan of this approach because I can't handle seeing all of the wasted fabric! Instead, I've learned to use the triangle size specified in the project instructions but stitch the diagonal edges with a *scant* seam allowance to produce a slightly oversized unit. Next, I position an acrylic ruler onto the unit, with the diagonal 45° line resting on the diagonal seam of the patchwork, and use a rotary cutter to trim away the excess fabric beyond the ruler's edge. Last,

Joining Borders

To easily join patchwork or single-fabric borders to a quilt top, I've learned to find the center of both the borders *and* the quilt top by folding them in half and finger-pressing the positions to mark them. I then match up the center creases and pin the layers together at this point. Next, I match and pin the layers together at each opposite end, ensuring the edges are flush. Last, I work from the center out to each end, pinning the edges at even intervals and easing in any size differences for a perfect fit. Finding the center and working outward is a technique I've used for years, and it gives me great results when joining borders (and large blocks or units, too!).

For large patchwork units that receive a lot of handling as they're pinned and stitched, the pins can sometimes wiggle free, requiring me to stop stitching and reposition them. I hate when that happens! To keep my units securely pinned, I use a technique I call pin-weaving. This simply means that at the beginning and end of the unit (where the pieces can receive a lot of stress), I weave the pin through the fabric *twice* instead of once, and also in a handful of additional positions at spaced intervals. With this little trick, the woven pins won't wiggle free and the patchwork stays secure.

Quick Fixes

If I complete a patchwork unit or block and discover that it finishes slightly too small in size, here's a quick little trick I use that will often eliminate the need for me to unsew and resew it. With my iron on a hot, dry setting, I anchor one edge of the patchwork right side up on my pressing surface with my hand, and then gently smooth the iron from the center outward, sliding it away from me to the opposite edge of the block. I then rotate the patchwork and repeat this step for each side. This simple step helps ensure the seam allowances are pressed completely open to the seam, and it can gently relax and stretch the fabric slightly to bring the block up to the correct size.

For patchwork that finishes slightly too large, I spray the unit lightly with Best Press or set my iron to the steam setting and carefully press the unit to slightly shrink the fibers of the fabric. This easy step can often eliminate the need to resew seams, and when combined with a small trim along the outer unit edges, it will produce finished patchwork in the needed size.

From time to time, even when I've used a neutral thread color in my sewing machine, some of the stitches may be visible after the seams have been pressed. When this happens, I use a Pigma Micron marker with a fine tip (usually in a brown or gray color) to place a tiny dot on the thread. This little trick helps the thread blend into the print of the fabric, and the stitches vanish!

When I'm busy stitching patchwork projects, I sometimes forget to change my sewing-machine needle as often as I should, and this can result in a dull point. Seeing an occasional thread pull in the print of my fabric is a big reminder that I've neglected to change my needle! To easily fix the resulting line that's now visible, I use the tip of a needle at the outermost end of the pull to gently drag the thread back toward the seamline. This quick step realigns the thread within the print, and the fabric looks good as new. And then I change the sewing-machine needle!

Finishing Touches

As I'm piecing my blocks I don't press them with steam, because this can make it difficult to make corrections. However, I do like to press the finished blocks well to firmly set the seams in place. My preferred method is to lay the block wrong side up on my pressing surface and give it a light misting of Best Press (plain water in a spray bottle will also work well). While the fabric is still damp, I bring a hot, dry iron down onto the block, letting it rest in place for a few seconds. I continue working across the block in this way to set the seam allowances in place, ensuring they're resting flat and in the intended direction. Once the pressing is complete from the back of the block, I flip it to the front and repeat the steps, misting again if I feel it will be helpful. This technique produces smooth, flat blocks, and I often repeat it after the top has been assembled for a beautiful finish across the entire project.

To prevent my quilt-top seam allowances from raveling during the quilting process, I lay the quilt on a table with the raw edge extending just beyond the table's edge. Next, I use the side edge of the table to steady my hand and slide it along the length of the quilt top to apply a thin line of liquid seam sealant (Fray Check works great!). When the fabric has dried (this only takes a moment or two), I reposition the quilt top and repeat until the entire perimeter of the quilt top has been protected.

For any finished quilt top with many seams along the outer perimeter, I use a straight sewing-machine stitch in the longest length to stay stitch approximately ⅛" from each raw edge. This simple step helps keep the sewn seams intact during the quilting process, whether by hand or machine, and the stay stitching will be hidden underneath the binding once the quilt is complete.

To me, the final (and best!) finishing touch is quilting your quilt. For several of the larger-scale projects in this book, an edge-to-edge quilting design can be an ideal choice—and don't forget to consider programmed designs as a convenient and cost-effective option! When I choose quilting designs for my quilts, I often think in terms of opposites. Softly curved, free-form quilting designs will complement patchwork with many straight lines and angles, whereas rounder patchwork shapes will benefit from the sense of order that straight stitched lines and cross-hatching can bring. Something to think about!

Quiltmaking Basics

You'll find a wealth of basic quiltmaking techniques in the section that follows, with the information provided in simple, approachable steps.

Prewashing Fabric

There are lots of opinions about whether fabrics should be prewashed before using them. My opinion is . . . it's totally a matter of personal preference! I choose not to prewash my fabrics because I like the extra bit of body and stability the fabric has in its purchased condition. For very strongly hued prints that might bleed color (such as red), I test the print by cutting a small piece of fabric and placing it in a bowl of warm water with a few drops of detergent, then laying it on layers of white paper towel to dry. If the print isn't colorfast, you'll see a tint of color on the paper towel. Even though you might love this print, you'll want to exclude it from your fabric stash.

If you do decide that prewashing is the right choice for you, it should be done consistently to ensure your prints for any given project have the same degree of shrinkage and weight. To prewash, I suggest doing so with prints of similar colors, using a mild detergent with no fragrance, and choosing a cold-water setting for your washing machine. After the fabric has been dried, you'll likely need to press it with a hot iron to remove wrinkles.

Rotary Cutting

Unless otherwise instructed, all pieces should be cut across the width of the fabric (from selvage to selvage). For quick and efficient cutting, I routinely fold my pressed fabric in half with the selvage edges together. (Please check out the tip on page 101 for prints with a pronounced gridded pattern or stripe.) For smaller-scale patchwork I often fold the fabric in half once more, but of course this will depend upon the size and number of pieces to be cut. Next, I lay the folded fabric on a cutting mat, make a cut to establish a straight edge, and cut my pieces, working outward from this point.

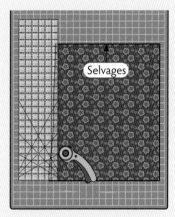

To cut half-square-triangle units from a single square or layered stack of squares, position your ruler diagonally across the square and use a rotary cutter to make the cut from corner to corner.

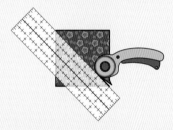

Pinning

I recommend pinning your patchwork at regular intervals, including the intersection of all sewn seams. To help eliminate bulky lumps, ensure the seams are lying flat and resting in the correct direction as they're pinned.

Machine Piecing

Unless otherwise instructed, always join your fabrics with right sides together using a ¼" seam allowance.

For projects with many pieces to be joined, chain piecing is the perfect way to increase your speed and save thread. Simply feed your patchwork through the sewing machine continuously without snipping the threads; after stitching, cut the threads between the units to separate them.

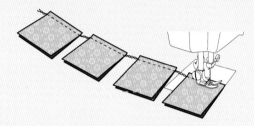

Pressing Seams

Pressing seams well is a *must* for accurate patchwork. I recommend using a hot, dry iron to press as follows.

1 Place the patchwork on your ironing surface with the fabric you wish to press toward (usually the darker print) on top. On the wrong side of the fabric, briefly bring your iron down onto the sewn seam to warm the fabric.

2 While the fabric is still warm, fold the top piece of fabric back to expose the right sides of the fabric. Run your fingernail along the sewn thread line to open the fabric all the way to the line of stitching; press the seam flat from the right side of the patchwork. The seam allowances will now lie under the fabric that was originally positioned on top.

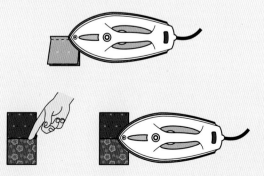

Pressing Triangle Units

For projects that call for stitch-and-fold triangles (made by folding open one corner of a diagonally stitched top square, as described in each applicable project), I recommend the following steps.

1 Fold the stitched top triangle back and align the corner with the corner of the bottom square or rectangle; press in place.

2 Trim away the layers of fabric beneath the top triangle, leaving a ¼" seam allowance.

Traditionally, the layers beneath the top triangle are trimmed *before* the unit is pressed, but I've found that my method of pressing and then trimming produces more accurate patchwork that seldom requires squaring up.

Finishing Techniques

There are many options available as you complete your project. The information that follows will help you make informed choices for a finished quilt that perfectly suits your preferences.

BATTING

For quilt tops sewn from prewashed fabrics, I suggest using polyester batting or a cotton/polyester blend; this will ensure minimal shrinkage when your quilt is laundered. If your quilt top was stitched from fabrics that weren't prewashed, I recommend cotton batting, particularly if you love the slightly puckered

look of vintage quilts. For best results, always follow the manufacturer's instructions for how densely to quilt and how to launder.

BACKING

I routinely cut and piece my quilt backings to be approximately 3" larger than my quilt top on all sides. Remember that prints with strong patterns will make your quilting less visible, while muted prints and solids will emphasize your quilting design. To prevent shadowing, it's generally best to use fabrics in colors similar to those in your quilt top.

BASTING

When it is time to prepare your project for the quilting process, the completed top can be layered with the batting and backing and stabilized for stitching using a thread- or pin-basting technique.

For smaller-sized projects, I love the convenience of sandwiching the layers together using basting spray, following the manufacturer's instructions.

MARKING QUILTING DESIGNS

Masking tape in various widths works beautifully as a guide for stitching straight quilting lines. More elaborate designs can be marked onto the top using a quilter's pencil or a fine-tipped water-soluble marker before the layers are basted together. Blue markers work well for light- and medium-hued fabrics, while white markers work perfectly for medium- and dark-hued prints. For a beautiful finish, always ensure your quilt features an abundant and evenly spaced amount of quilting.

MACHINE QUILTING

For in-depth machine-quilting instructions, please refer to *Pat Sloan's Teach Me to Machine Quilt* or *The Ultimate Guide to Machine Quilting* by Angela Walters and Christa Watson.

Chubby Binding

Traditionally, a 2½"-wide French-fold binding is used to finish most quilts. For my quilts, I prefer a less conventional binding using 2"-wide strips that result in a traditional look while producing a "chubby" border to frame the backing and add a pop of color. An added benefit is that this method reduces bulk at the mitered corners.

For my chubby-binding method, you'll need a bias-tape maker designed to produce 1"-wide, double-fold tape. For most of my quilts, I prefer to use binding strips that have been cut on the straight of grain, rather than the bias, because I feel this gives my quilt edges added stability—but this is entirely up to you. For scrappy bindings pieced from many prints cut from different lengths, I love the look achieved when the strips are joined end to end using straight seams.

1 Cut the strips 2" wide and join them end to end without pressing the seam allowances. Next, slide the pieced strip through the bias-tape maker, pressing the folds with a hot, dry iron as they emerge so the raw edges meet in the center. As the tape maker slides along the pieced strip, the seams will automatically be directed to one side as they are pressed, resulting in one less step!

2 Unfold the strip along the top edge only. Turn the beginning raw end under ½" and finger-press the fold. Beginning on one side of the quilt top (not a corner), align the *unfolded* raw edge of the binding with the raw edge of the quilt. Use a ¼" seam allowance to stitch the binding along the raw edges. Stop sewing ¼" from the first corner and add two or three backstitches. Clip the thread and remove the quilt from under the presser foot.

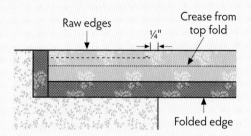

3 Make a fold in the binding, bringing it up and back down onto itself to square the corner. Rotate the quilt 90° and reposition it under the presser foot. Resume sewing at the top edge of the quilt, continuing around the perimeter in this manner.

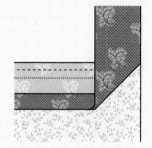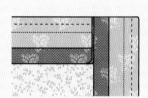

4 When you approach your starting point, cut the end to extend approximately 1" beyond the folded edge and complete the stitching.

5 Bring the wide folded edge of the binding to the back and hand stitch it in place, including the mitered folds at the corners. The raw end of the strip will now be encased within the binding.

Attaching a Quilt Label

To document your work, remember to prepare a fabric quilt label including any information you'd like to share, and then hand stitch it to the back of your quilt.

About the Author

After falling in love with a sampler quilt pattern in the late 1990s, Kim impulsively purchased it, taught herself the steps needed to make it, and then realized she was smitten with quiltmaking. As her newfound passion blossomed into a full-time career, Kim began publishing her original designs, traveling nationally to teach her approachable quiltmaking methods, and ultimately designing fabrics . . . a dream come true for a girl who once wondered if she had what it took to make a single quilt!

Using modern time-saving techniques, such as the easy invisible-machine-appliqué method she's known for, enables Kim to be prolific in her quiltmaking, and there's always something new in the works. Her very favorite quilts feature scrappy color schemes sewn from a mix of richly hued prints, and her designs often blend traditionally inspired patchwork with appliqué designs.

In addition to authoring numerous books, including her "Simple" series with Martingale, Kim continues to design quilting fabric collections and Simple Whatnots Club projects in her signature scrap-basket style for Henry Glass & Co.

After retiring from an extensive travel and teaching schedule in 2015, Kim now spends her days at home doing what she loves most—designing quilts and fabrics, baking, stitching, gardening, and being a nana to her grandies.